Air Fryer Meals For Two

Teo .L Mill

Introduction

This book offers a delightful array of recipes designed for the convenience and enjoyment of cooking with an air fryer. From breakfast to dessert, this cookbook provides a diverse selection of mouth-watering dishes that cater specifically to serving two.

In the breakfast section, you'll find tempting options like Tasty Baked Eggs, Breakfast Egg Bowls, and the ever-popular Egg Muffins. The recipes span a spectrum of flavors, from Rustic Breakfast to Sweet Breakfast Casserole, ensuring a delightful start to your day without the hassle of large portions.

The lunch section offers an equally enticing array of choices, such as Lunch Egg Rolls, Tuna and Zucchini Tortillas, and Chicken Sandwiches. These recipes are crafted to satisfy your midday cravings with quick and flavorful options that suit a party of two.

For sides and snacks, the cookbook presents an assortment of delectable choices ranging from Potato Wedges to Zucchini Fries, offering a perfect complement to any main course. The variety extends to vegetable side dishes like Brussels Sprouts, Roasted Pumpkin, and Garlic Potatoes, providing a diverse selection to suit any palate.

The seafood and meat section introduces an exciting collection of recipes featuring a variety of proteins, including Salmon Party Patties, Cod Steaks with Plum Sauce, and Flavored Rib Eye Steak. These recipes showcase the versatility of the air fryer in preparing succulent and flavorful main dishes.

Dessert lovers will be delighted by the sweet treats offered in the final section, featuring options like Banana Cake, Cheesecake, and Cocoa Cake. The dessert section caters to the sweet tooth of two, ensuring that you can indulge without excess.

In essence, this book is a culinary treasure trove that simplifies the art of air frying, presenting a collection of recipes that balance flavor, convenience, and portion control. Whether you're a novice in the kitchen or an experienced chef, this cookbook provides a delightful journey through the possibilities of cooking for two with an air fryer.

Contents

Tasty Baked Eggs

Preparation time: 10 minutes **Cooking time:** 20 minutes
Servings: 4

Ingredients:

- ➢ 4 eggs
- ➢ 1 pound baby spinach, torn
- ➢ 7 oz ham, chop
- ➢ 4 tbsp milk
- ➢ 1 tbsp olive oil
- ➢ Cooking spray
- ➢ Salt and black pepper to the taste

Directions:

1. Heat the oil in a pan over medium heat, then add the baby spinach and toss for a few minutes before turning off the heat.
2. Cooking spray 4 ramekins and divide baby spinach and ham among them.
3. Crack an egg into each ramekin, split the milk, season with salt and pepper, and bake for 20 minutes in a preheated air fryer at 350 degrees F.
4. Breakfast can be made with baked eggs. Enjoy!

Nutrition: 321 calories, 6 grams of fat, 8 grams of fiber, 15 grams of carbohydrates, and 12 grams of protein

Breakfast Egg Bowls

Preparation time: 10 minutes **Cooking time:** 20 minutes **Servings:** 4

Ingredients:

- ➤ 4 dinner rolls, tops cut off and insides scooped out
- ➤ 4 tbsp heavy cream
- ➤ 4 eggs
- ➤ 4 tbsp mixed chives and parsley
- ➤ Salt and black pepper to the taste
- ➤ 4 tbsp parmesan, grated

Directions:

1. On a baking sheet, arrange dinner rolls and crack an egg into each one.
2. In each roll, divide the heavy cream and mixed herbs and season with salt and pepper.
3. Sprinkle parmesan cheese on top of the rolls before placing them in your air fryer and cooking for 20 minutes at 350 degrees F.
4. Serve your bread bowls for breakfast by dividing them among plates. Enjoy!

Nutrition: 238 calories, 4 grams of fat, 7 grams of fiber, 14 grams of carbohydrates, and 7 grams of protein

Delicious Breakfast Soufflé

Preparation time: 10 minutes **Cooking time:** 8 minutes
Servings: 4

Ingredients:

- ➢ 4 eggs, whisked
- ➢ 4 tbsp heavy cream
- ➢ A pinch of red chili pepper, crushed
- ➢ 2 tbsp parsley, chop
- ➢ 2 tbsp chives, chop
- ➢ Salt and black pepper to the taste

Directions:

1. Combine eggs, salt, pepper, heavy cream, red chili pepper, parsley, and chives in a mixing bowl, stir well, and divide among four soufflé plates.
2. Cook soufflés at 350 degrees F for 8 minutes after arranging dishes in your air fryer.
3. Serve them immediately. Enjoy!

Nutrition: 300 calories, 7 grams of fat, 9 grams of fiber, 15 grams of carbohydrates, and 6 grams of protein

Air Fried Sandwich

Preparation time: 10 minutes **Cooking time:** 6 minutes
Servings: 2

Ingredients:

- ➢ 2 English muffins, halved
- ➢ 2 eggs
- ➢ 2 bacon strips
- ➢ Salt and black pepper to the taste

Directions:

1. In your air fryer, crack eggs, top with bacon, cover, and cook for 6 minutes at 392 degrees F.
2. Heat the English muffin halves in the microwave for a few seconds, then split the eggs between two half, top with bacon, season with salt and pepper, and serve for breakfast. Enjoy!

Nutrition: 261 calories, 5 grams of fat, 8 grams of fiber, 12 grams of carbohydrates, and 4 grams of protein

Rustic Breakfast

Preparation time: 10 minutes **Cooking time:** 13 minutes **Servings:** 4

Ingredients:

- ➢ 7 oz baby spinach
- ➢ 8 chestnuts mushrooms, halved
- ➢ 8 tomatoes, halved
- ➢ 1 garlic clove, minced
- ➢ 4 chipolatas
- ➢ 4 bacon slices, chop
- ➢ Salt and black pepper to the taste
- ➢ 4 eggs
- ➢ Cooking spray

Directions:

1. Add the tomatoes, garlic, and mushrooms to a frying pan that has been greased with the oil.
2. Add the bacon and chipolatas at the end, as well as the spinach and cracked eggs.

3. Season with salt and pepper, then place the pan in the air fryer's frying basket and cook for 13 minutes at 350°F.
4. Serve for breakfast by dividing the mixture among dishes. Enjoy!

Nutrition: 312 calories, 6 grams of fat, 8 grams of fiber, 15 grams of carbohydrates, 5 grams of protein.

Egg Muffins

Preparation time: 10 minutes **Cooking time:** 15 minutes
Servings: 4

Ingredients:

- ➤ 1 egg
- ➤ 2 tbsp olive oil
- ➤ 3 tbsp milk
- ➤ 3.5 oz white flour
- ➤ 1 tbsp baking powder
- ➤ 2 oz parmesan, grated
- ➤ A splash of Worcestershire sauce

Directions:

1. Combine egg, flour, oil, baking powder, milk, Worcestershire, and parmesan in a mixing dish, whisk well, and divide among four silicon muffin cups.
2. Place cups in the frying basket of your air fryer, cover, and cook for 15 minutes at 392 degrees F.
3. For breakfast, serve warm. Enjoy!

Nutrition: 251 calories, 6 grams of fat, 8 grams of fiber, 9 grams of carbohydrates, 3 grams of protein

Polenta Bites

Preparation time: 10 minutes **Cooking time:** 20 minutes
Servings: 4

Ingredients:

For the polenta:

- ➢ 1 tbsp butter
- ➢ 1 cup cornmeal
- ➢ 3 cups water
- ➢ Salt and black pepper to the taste

For the polenta bites:

- ➢ 2 tbsp powdered sugar
- ➢ Cooking spray

Directions:

1. In a saucepan, combine water, cornmeal, butter, salt, and pepper; stir to combine; bring to a boil over medium heat; cook for 10 minutes; remove from heat; whisk once more; chill until cold.
2. Scoop 1 tablespoon of polenta, roll it into a ball, and set it on a work surface.
3. Repeat with the remaining polenta, then place all of the balls in the air fryer's cooking basket, spray with cooking spray, cover, and cook for 8 minutes at 380 degrees F.
4. Serve polenta bits for breakfast by arranging them on plates and sprinkling sugar over them. Enjoy!

Nutrition: 231 calories, 7 grams of fat, 8 grams of fiber, 12 grams of carbohydrates, and 4 grams of protein

Delicious Breakfast Potatoes

Preparation time: 10 minutes **Cooking time:** 35 minutes
Servings: 4

Ingredients:

- ➤ 2 tbsp olive oil
- ➤ 3 potatoes, cubed
- ➤ 1 yellow onion, chop
- ➤ 1 red bell pepper, chop
- ➤ Salt and black pepper to the taste
- ➤ 1 tsp garlic powder
- ➤ 1 tsp sweet paprika
- ➤ 1 tsp onion powder

Directions:

1. Using olive oil, grease the basket of your air fryer, add the potatoes, mix, and season with salt and pepper.
2. Toss in the onion, bell pepper, garlic powder, paprika, and onion powder, cover, and cook for 30 minutes at 370 degrees F.
3. Serve the potato mixture for breakfast on plates. Enjoy!

Nutrition: 214 calories, 6 grams of fat, 8 grams of fiber, 15 grams of carbohydrates, and 4 grams of protein

Tasty Cinnamon Toast

Preparation time: 10 minutes **Cooking time:** 5 minutes
Servings: 6

Ingredients:

- ➤ 1 stick butter, soft
- ➤ 12 bread slices
- ➤ 1/2 cup sugar
- ➤ 1 and 1/2 tsp vanilla extract
- ➤ 1 and 1/2 tsp cinnamon powder

Directions:

1. Whisk together soft butter, sugar, vanilla, and cinnamon in a mixing dish.
2. Spread this on bread pieces, toss them in the air fryer, and cook for 5 minutes at 400 degrees F. Divide among plates and serve for breakfast. Enjoy!

Nutrition: 221 calories, 4 grams of fat, 7 grams of fiber, 12 grams of carbohydrates, and 8 grams of protein

Delicious Potato Hash

Preparation time: 10 minutes **Cooking time:** 25 minutes
Servings: 4

Ingredients:

- ➤ 1 and 1/2 potatoes, cubed
- ➤ 1 yellow onion, chop
- ➤ 2 tsp olive oil
- ➤ 1 green bell pepper, chop
- ➤ Salt and black pepper to the taste
- ➤ 1/2 tsp thyme, dried
- ➤ 2 eggs

Directions:

1. Preheat your air fryer to 350°F, add the oil, heat it up, then add the onion, bell pepper, salt, and pepper, stir, and cook for 5 minutes.
2. Stir in the potatoes, thyme, and eggs, then cover and bake for 20 minutes at 360 degrees F.
3. Serve for breakfast by dividing the mixture among dishes. Enjoy!

Nutrition: 241 calories, 4 grams of fat, 7 grams of fiber, 12 grams of carbohydrates, and 7 grams of protein

Sweet Breakfast Casserole

Preparation time: 10 minutes **Cooking time:** 30 minutes
Servings: 4

Ingredients:

- ➢ 3 tbsp brown sugar
- ➢ 4 tbsp butter
- ➢ 2 tbsp white sugar
- ➢ 1/2 tsp cinnamon powder
- ➢ 1/2 cup flour

For the casserole:

- ➢ 2 eggs
- ➢ 2 tbsp white sugar
- ➢ 2 and 1/2 cups white flour
- ➢ 1 tsp baking soda
- ➢ 1 tsp baking powder

- ➢ 2 eggs
- ➢ 1/2 cup milk
- ➢ 2 cups buttermilk
- ➢ 4 tbsp butter
- ➢ Zest from 1 lemon, grated
- ➢ 1 and 2/3 cup blueberries

Directions:

1. Combine 2 tbsp white sugar, 2 and 1/2 cups white flour, baking powder, baking soda, 2 eggs, milk, buttermilk, 4 tbsp butter, lemon zest, and blueberries in a mixing bowl, whisk well, and pour into an air fryer-safe pan.
2. Mix 3 tbsp brown sugar with 2 tbsp white sugar, 4 tbsp butter, 1/2 cup flour, and cinnamon in a separate dish until a crumble forms, then pour over blueberries.
3. Bake for 30 minutes at 300 degrees F in a preheated air fryer.
4. Serve for breakfast by dividing the mixture among dishes. Enjoy!

Nutrition: 214 calories, 5 grams of fat, 8 grams of fiber, 12 grams of carbohydrates, and 5 grams of protein

Eggs Casserole

Preparation time: 10 minutes **Cooking time:** 25 minutes
Servings: 6

Ingredients:

- ➢ 1 pound turkey, ground
- ➢ 1 tbsp olive oil

- ➤ 1/2 tsp chili powder
- ➤ 12 eggs
- ➤ 1 sweet potato, cubed
- ➤ 1 cup baby spinach
- ➤ Salt and black pepper to the taste
- ➤ 2 tomatoes, chop for serving

Directions:

1. In a mixing dish, whisk together eggs, salt, pepper, chili powder, potato, spinach, turkey, and sweet potato.
2. Preheat your air fryer to 350 degrees F, then add the oil and heat again.
3. Add the egg mixture to your air fryer, spread it out, cover, and cook for 25 minutes.
4. Serve for breakfast by dividing the mixture among dishes. Enjoy!

Nutrition: 300 calories, 5 grams of fat, 8 grams of fiber, 13 grams of carbohydrate, and 6 grams of protein

Sausage, Eggs and Cheese Mix

Preparation time: 10 minutes **Cooking time:** 20 minutes
Servings: 4

Ingredients:

- ➤ 10 oz sausages, cooked and crumbled
- ➤ 1 cup cheddar cheese, shredded
- ➤ 1 cup mozzarella cheese, shredded
- ➤ 8 eggs, whisked
- ➤ 1 cup milk

- ➢ Salt and black pepper to the taste
- ➢ Cooking spray

Directions:

1. Whisk together sausages, cheese, mozzarella, eggs, milk, salt, and pepper in a mixing bowl.
2. Preheat your air fryer to 380°F, spray it with frying oil, then add the eggs and sausage mixture and cook for 20 minutes.
3. Serve by dividing the mixture among plates. Enjoy!

Nutrition: 320 calories, 6 grams of fat, 8 grams of fiber, 12 grams of carbohydrates, and 5 grams of protein

Cheese Air Fried Bake

Preparation time: 10 minutes **Cooking time:** 20 minutes
Servings: 4

Ingredients:

- ➢ 4 bacon slices, cooked and crumbled
- ➢ 2 cups milk
- ➢ 2 and 1/2 cups cheddar cheese, shredded
- ➢ 1 pound breakfast sausage, casings removed and chop
- ➢ 2 eggs
- ➢ 1/2 tsp onion powder
- ➢ Salt and black pepper to the taste
- ➢ 3 tbsp parsley, chop
- ➢ Cooking spray

Directions:

1. Whisk together eggs, milk, cheese, onion powder, salt, pepper, and parsley in a mixing bowl.
2. Spray your air fryer with cooking spray, preheat to 320°F, then add the bacon and sausage.
3. Cook for 20 minutes after adding the egg mixture and spreading it out.
4. Serve by dividing the mixture among plates. Enjoy!

Nutrition: 214 calories, 5 grams of fat, 8 grams of fiber, 12 grams of carbohydrates, and 12 grams of protein

Biscuits Casserole

Preparation time: 10 minutes **Cooking time:** 15 minutes **Servings:** 8

Ingredients:

- ➤ 12 oz biscuits, quartered
- ➤ 3 tbsp flour
- ➤ 1/2 pound sausage, chop
- ➤ A pinch of salt and black pepper
- ➤ 2 and 1/2 cups milk
- ➤ Cooking spray

Directions:

1. Heat your air fryer to 350 degrees F after spraying it with cooking spray.
2. Add the biscuits to the bottom of the pan and toss with the meat.
3. Toss in the flour, milk, salt, and pepper, and simmer for 15 minutes.

4. Serve for breakfast by dividing the mixture among dishes. Enjoy!

Nutrition: 321 calories, 4 grams of fat, 7 grams of fiber, 12 grams of carbohydrate, and 5 grams of protein

Turkey Burrito

Preparation time: 10 minutes **Cooking time:** 10 minutes **Servings:** 2

Ingredients:

- ➢ 4 slices turkey breast already cooked
- ➢ 1/2 red bell pepper, sliced
- ➢ 2 eggs
- ➢ 1 small avocado, peeled, pitted and sliced
- ➢ 2 tbsp salsa
- ➢ Salt and black pepper to the taste
- ➢ 1/8 cup mozzarella cheese, grated
- ➢ Tortillas for serving

Directions:

1. Whisk eggs in a basin with salt and pepper to taste, then pour into a pan and set in the air fryer's basket.
2. Cook for 5 minutes at 400 degrees F, then remove the pan from the fryer and transfer the eggs to a platter.
3. Arrange tortillas on a work surface, then divide eggs, turkey meat, bell pepper, cheese, salsa, and avocado among them.
4. After lining your air fryer with tin foil, roll your burritos and lay them in it.

5. Heat the burritos for 3 minutes at 300 degrees F, then divide them among plates and serve. Enjoy!

Nutrition: 349 calories, 23 grams of fat, 11 grams of fiber, 20 grams of carbohydrates, and 21 grams of protein

Tofu Scramble

Preparation time: 5 minutes **Cooking time:** 30 minutes
Servings: 4

Ingredients:

- ➢ 2 tbsp soy sauce
- ➢ 1 tofu block, cubed
- ➢ 1 tsp turmeric, ground
- ➢ 2 tbsp extra virgin olive oil
- ➢ 4 cups broccoli florets
- ➢ 1/2 tsp onion powder
- ➢ 1/2 tsp garlic powder
- ➢ 2 and 1/2 cup red potatoes, cubed
- ➢ 1/2 cup yellow onion, chop
- ➢ Salt and black pepper to the taste

Directions:

1. In a bowl, combine tofu, 1 tablespoon oil, salt, pepper, soy sauce, garlic powder, onion powder, turmeric, and onion; stir well and set away.
2. Toss potatoes with the remaining oil, a pinch of salt, and pepper in a separate bowl to coat.
3. Preheat your air fryer at 350 degrees F and bake potatoes for 15 minutes, shaking once halfway through.

4. Bake for 15 minutes in your air fryer with the tofu and marinade.
5. Cook for another 5 minutes in the fryer with the broccoli.
6. Serve immediately. Enjoy!

Nutrition: 140 calories, 4 grams of fat, 3 grams of fiber, 10 grams of carbohydrates, 14 grams of protein

Oatmeal Casserole

Preparation time: 10 minutes **Cooking time:** 20 minutes
Servings: 8

Ingredients:

- ➢ 2 cups rolled oats
- ➢ 1 tsp baking powder
- ➢ 1/3 cup brown sugar
- ➢ 1 tsp cinnamon powder
- ➢ 1/2 cup chocolate chips
- ➢ 2/3 cup blueberries
- ➢ 1 banana, peeled and mashed
- ➢ 2 cups milk
- ➢ 1 eggs
- ➢ 2 tbsp butter
- ➢ 1 tsp vanilla extract
- ➢ Cooking spray

Directions:

1. Stir together the sugar, baking powder, cinnamon, chocolate chips, blueberries, and banana in a mixing dish.

2. In a separate dish, whisk together the eggs, vanilla essence, and butter.
3. Preheat your air fryer to 320°F, coat it with cooking spray, and sprinkle oats on the bottom.
4. Toss in the cinnamon and egg mixture and simmer for 20 minutes.
5. Stir in the other ingredients, divide into dishes, and serve for breakfast. Enjoy!

Nutrition: 300 calories, 4 grams of fat, 7 grams of fiber, 12 grams of carbohydrates, and 10 grams of protein

Ham Breakfast

Preparation time: 10 minutes **Cooking time:** 15 minutes
Servings: 6

Ingredients:

➢ 6 cups French bread, cubed
➢ 4 oz green chilies, chop
➢ 10 oz ham, cubed
➢ 4 oz cheddar cheese, shredded
➢ 2 cups milk
➢ 5 eggs
➢ 1 tbsp mustard
➢ Salt and black pepper to the taste
➢ Cooking spray

Directions:

1. Preheat your air fryer to 350°F and coat it with cooking spray.

2. In a mixing dish, whisk together the eggs, milk, cheese, mustard, salt, and pepper.
3. In your air fryer, combine bread cubes, chiles, and ham.
4. Cook for 15 minutes after adding the egg mixture and spreading it out.
5. Serve by dividing the mixture among plates. Enjoy!

Nutrition: 200 calories, 5 grams of fat, 6 grams of fiber, 12 grams of carbohydrates, 14 grams of protein

Tomato and Bacon Breakfast

Preparation time: 10 minutes **Cooking time:** 30 minutes **Servings:** 6

Ingredients:

➤ 1 pound white bread, cubed
➤ 1 pound smoked bacon, cooked and chop
➤ 1/4 cup olive oil
➤ 1 yellow onion, chop
➤ 28 oz canned tomatoes, chop
➤ 1/2 tsp red pepper, crushed
➤ 1/2 pound cheddar, shredded
➤ 2 tbsp chives, chop
➤ 1/2 pound Monterey jack, shredded
➤ 2 tbsp stock
➤ Salt and black pepper to the taste
➤ 8 eggs, whisked

Directions:

1. Heat the oil in your air fryer to 350 degrees Fahrenheit.

2. Stir in the bread, bacon, onion, tomatoes, red pepper, and stock.
3. Cook for 20 minutes with the eggs, cheddar, and Monterey jack cheeses.
4. Serve by dividing among dishes and garnishing with chives. Enjoy!

Nutrition: 231 calories, 5 grams of fat, 7 grams of fiber, 12 grams of carbohydrates, and 4 grams of protein

Tasty Hash

Preparation time: 10 minutes **Cooking time:** 15 minutes **Servings:** 6

Ingredients:

- ➤ 16 oz hash browns
- ➤ 1/4 cup olive oil
- ➤ 1/2 tsp paprika
- ➤ 1/2 tsp garlic powder
- ➤ Salt and black pepper to the taste
- ➤ 1 egg, whisked
- ➤ 2 tbsp chives, chop
- ➤ 1 cup cheddar, shredded

Directions:

1. Heat the oil in your air fryer to 350 degrees Fahrenheit before adding the hash browns.
2. Toss in the paprika, garlic powder, salt, and pepper, and simmer for another 15 minutes.

3. Toss in the cheddar and chives, then divide into plates. Enjoy!

Nutrition: 213 calories, 7 grams of fat, 8 grams of fiber, 12 grams of carbohydrates, and 4 grams of protein

Creamy Hash Browns

Preparation time: 10 minutes **Cooking time:** 20 minutes **Servings:** 6

Ingredients:

- ➤ 2 pounds hash browns
- ➤ 1 cup whole milk
- ➤ 8 bacon slices, chop
- ➤ 9 oz cream cheese
- ➤ 1 yellow onion, chop
- ➤ 1 cup cheddar cheese, shredded
- ➤ 6 green onions, chop
- ➤ Salt and black pepper to the taste
- ➤ 6 eggs
- ➤ Cooking spray

Directions:

1. Preheat your air fryer to 350°F and coat it with cooking spray.
2. In a mixing bowl, whisk together eggs, milk, cream cheese, cheddar cheese, bacon, onion, salt, and pepper.
3. Place hash browns in the air fryer, top with egg mixture, and cook for 20 minutes.
4. Serve by dividing the mixture among plates. Enjoy!

Nutrition: 241 calories, 6 grams of fat, 9 grams of fiber, 8 grams of carbohydrates, and 12 grams of protein

Blackberry French Toast

Preparation time: 10 minutes **Cooking time:** 20 minutes
Servings: 6

Ingredients:

- ➢ 1 cup blackberry jam, warm
- ➢ 12 oz bread loaf, cubed
- ➢ 8 oz cream cheese, cubed
- ➢ 4 eggs
- ➢ 1 tsp cinnamon powder
- ➢ 2 cups half and half
- ➢ 1/2 cup brown sugar
- ➢ 1 tsp vanilla extract
- ➢ Cooking spray

Directions:

1. Preheat your air fryer to 300 degrees F after spraying it with cooking spray.
2. On the bottom, spread blueberry jam, then stack half of the bread cubes, cream cheese, then the rest of the bread.
3. Combine eggs, half-and-half, cinnamon, sugar, and vanilla in a mixing dish, beat well, and pour over bread mixture.
4. Cook for 20 minutes, then divide into plates for breakfast. Enjoy!

Nutrition: 215 calories, 6 grams of fat, 9 grams of fiber, 16 grams of carbohydrates, and 6 grams of protein

Lunch Egg Rolls

Preparation time: 10 minutes **Cooking time:** 15 minutes
Servings: 4

Ingredients:

- ➤ 1/2 cup mushrooms, chop
- ➤ 1/2 cup carrots, grated
- ➤ 1/2 cup zucchini, grated
- ➤ 2 green onions, chop
- ➤ 2 tbsp soy sauce
- ➤ 8 egg roll wrappers
- ➤ 1 eggs, whisked
- ➤ 1 tbsp cornstarch

Directions:

1. Stir carrots, mushrooms, zucchini, green onions, and soy sauce together in a basin.
2. Arrange egg roll wrappers on a work surface, divide the veggie mixture among them, and roll tightly.
3. Mix cornstarch and egg in a bowl, whisk well, then brush this mixture over the eggs rolls.
4. Seal the edges, then set all of the rolls in your warmed air fryer and cook for 15 minutes at 370 degrees F.
5. Serve them for lunch by arranging them on a dish. Enjoy!

Nutrition: 172 calories, 6 grams of fat, 6 grams of fiber, 8 grams of carbohydrates, and 7 grams of protein

Veggie Toast

Preparation time: 10 minutes **Cooking time:** 15 minutes
Servings: 4

Ingredients:

- ➤ 1 red bell pepper, cut into thin strips
- ➤ 1 cup cremimi mushrooms, sliced
- ➤ 1 yellow squash, chop
- ➤ 2 green onions, sliced
- ➤ 1 tbsp olive oil
- ➤ 4 bread slices
- ➤ 2 tbsp butter, soft
- ➤ 1/2 cup goat cheese, crumbled

Directions:

1. Toss red bell pepper with mushrooms, squash, green onions, and oil in a bowl, then add to your air fryer and cook for 10 minutes at 350 degrees F, shaking the fryer once.
2. Spread butter on bread pieces, set in air fryer, and cook for 5 minutes at 350 degrees F.
3. Serve for lunch by dividing the veggie mixture among the bread slices and topping with crumbled cheese. Enjoy!

Nutrition: 152 calories, 3 grams of fat, 4 grams of fiber, 7 grams of carbohydrates, 2 grams of protein

Stuffed Mushrooms

Preparation time: 10 minutes **Cooking time:** 20 minutes
Servings: 4

Ingredients:

- ➢ 4 big Portobello mushroom caps
- ➢ 1 tbsp olive oil
- ➢ 1/4 cup ricotta cheese
- ➢ 5 tbsp parmesan, grated
- ➢ 1 cup spinach, torn
- ➢ 1/3 cup bread crumbs
- ➢ 1/4 tsp rosemary, chop

Directions:

1. Rub the mushroom caps with the oil, then place them in the air fryer basket and cook for 2 minutes at 350 degrees F.
2. Meanwhile, combine half of the parmesan, ricotta, spinach, rosemary, and bread crumbs in a mixing dish and stir well.
3. Stuff the mushrooms with the mixture, top with the remaining parmesan, and cook at 350 degrees F for 10 minutes in the air fryer basket.
4. For lunch, divide them among plates and serve with a side salad. Enjoy!

Nutrition: 152 calories, 4 grams of fat, 7 grams of fiber, 9 grams of carbohydrates, and 5 grams of protein

Quick Lunch Pizzas

Preparation time: 10 minutes **Cooking time:** 7 minutes
Servings: 4

Ingredients:

- ➢ 4 pitas
- ➢ 1 tbsp olive oil
- ➢ 3/4 cup pizza sauce
- ➢ 4 oz jarred mushrooms, sliced
- ➢ 1/2 tsp basil, dried
- ➢ 2 green onions, chop
- ➢ 2 cup mozzarella, grated
- ➢ 1 cup grape tomatoes, sliced

Directions:

1. On each pita bread, spread pizza sauce, green onions, and basil, divide mushrooms, and top with cheese.
2. Arrange pita pizzas in your air fryer and cook for 7 minutes at 400 degrees F.
3. Serve each pizza with tomato slices on top, divided among plates. Enjoy!

Nutrition: 200 calories, 4 grams of fat, 6 grams of fiber, 7 grams of carbohydrates, and 3 grams of protein

Lunch Gnocchi

Preparation time: 10 minutes **Cooking time:** 17 minutes
Servings: 4

Ingredients:

- ➢ 1 yellow onion, chop

- ➤ 1 tbsp olive oil
- ➤ 3 garlic cloves, minced
- ➤ 16 oz gnocchi
- ➤ 1/4 cup parmesan, grated
- ➤ 8 oz spinach pesto

Directions:

1. Grease the pan of your air fryer with olive oil, toss in the gnocchi, onion, and garlic, and cook at 400 degrees F for 10 minutes.
2. Toss in the pesto and cook for another 7 minutes at 350 degrees F.
3. Serve for lunch by dividing the mixture among plates. Enjoy!

Nutrition: 200 calories, 4 grams of fat, 4 grams of fiber, 12 grams of carbohydrates, and 4 grams of protein

Tuna and Zucchini Tortillas

Preparation time: 10 minutes **Cooking time:** 10 minutes
Servings: 4

Ingredients:

- ➤ 4 corn tortillas
- ➤ 4 tbsp butter, soft
- ➤ 6 oz canned tuna, drained
- ➤ 1 cup zucchini, shredded
- ➤ 1/3 cup mayonnaise
- ➤ 2 tbsp mustard
- ➤ 1 cup cheddar cheese, grated

Directions:

1. Spread butter over tortillas, set them in the basket of your air fryer, and cook for 3 minutes at 400 degrees F.
2. Meanwhile, combine tuna, zucchini, mayo, and mustard in a mixing dish and whisk well.
3. Divide the mixture among the tortillas, top with cheese, roll them up, and place them back in the air fryer basket to cook for another 4 minutes at 400 degrees F.
4. Serve at lunchtime. Enjoy!

Nutrition: 162 calories, 4 grams of fat, 8 grams of fiber, 9 grams of carbohydrates, and 4 grams of protein

Squash Fritters

Preparation time: 10 minutes **Cooking time:** 7 minutes
Servings: 4

Ingredients:

- ➤ 3 oz cream cheese
- ➤ 1 egg, whisked
- ➤ 1/2 tsp oregano, dried
- ➤ A pinch of salt and black pepper
- ➤ 1 yellow summer squash, grated
- ➤ 1/3 cup carrot, grated
- ➤ 2/3 cup bread crumbs
- ➤ 2 tbsp olive oil

Directions:

1. Combine cream cheese, salt, pepper, oregano, egg, breadcrumbs, carrots, and squash in a mixing dish and toss well.
2. Form medium patties from the mixture and brush with the oil.
3. Cook the squash patties in your air fryer for 7 minutes at 400 degrees F.
4. You can eat them for lunch. Enjoy!

Nutrition: 200 calories, 4 grams of fat, 7 grams of fiber, 8 grams of carbohydrates, and 6 grams of protein

Lunch Shrimp Croquettes

Preparation time: 10 minutes **Cooking time:** 8 minutes
Servings: 4

Ingredients:

- ➤ 2/3 pound shrimp, cooked, peeled, deveined and chop
- ➤ 1 and 1/2 cups bread crumbs
- ➤ 1 egg, whisked
- ➤ 2 tbsp lemon juice
- ➤ 3 green onions, chop
- ➤ 1/2 tsp basil, dried
- ➤ Salt and black pepper to the taste
- ➤ 2 tbsp olive oil

Directions:

1. Combine half of the bread crumbs, the egg, and the lemon juice in a mixing dish and toss well.

2. Stir in the green onions, basil, salt, and pepper, as well as the shrimp.
3. Mix the remaining bread crumbs with the oil in a separate bowl and toss thoroughly.
4. Form round balls out of the shrimp mixture, dredge them in bread crumbs, and cook for 8 minutes at 400 degrees F in a preheated air fryer.
5. For lunch, serve them with a dip. Enjoy!

Nutrition: 142 calories, 4 grams of fat, 6 grams of fiber, 9 grams of carbohydrates, and 4 grams of protein

Lunch Special Pancake

Preparation time: 10 minutes **Cooking time:** 10 minutes
Servings: 2

Ingredients:

- ➤ 1 tbsp butter
- ➤ 3 eggs, whisked
- ➤ 1/2 cup flour
- ➤ 1/2 cup milk
- ➤ 1 cup salsa
- ➤ 1 cup small shrimp, peeled and deveined

Directions:

1. Preheat your air fryer to 400 degrees F, then add 1 tablespoon butter to the fryer's pan and melt it.
2. In a mixing bowl, whisk together the eggs, flour, and milk. Pour into the air fryer pan, spread out, and cook for 12 minutes at 350 degrees.

3. Combine the shrimp and salsa in a bowl, whisk to combine, and serve on the side with your pancake. Enjoy!

Nutrition: 200 calories, 6 grams of fat, 8 grams of fiber, 12 grams of carbohydrates, and 4 grams of protein

Scallops and Dill

Preparation time: 10 minutes **Cooking time:** 5 minutes
Servings: 4

Ingredients:

- ➤ 1 pound sea scallops, debearded
- ➤ 1 tbsp lemon juice
- ➤ 1 tsp dill, chop
- ➤ 2 tsp olive oil
- ➤ Salt and black pepper to the taste

Directions:

1. Combine scallops, dill, oil, salt, pepper, and lemon juice in an air fryer, cover, and cook at 360 degrees F for 5 minutes.
2. Discard the ones that haven't been opened, then divide the scallops and dill sauce among plates and serve for lunch. Enjoy!

Nutrition: 152 calories, 4 grams of fat, 7 grams of fiber, 19 grams of carbohydrate, and 4 grams of protein

Chicken Sandwiches

Preparation time: 10 minutes **Cooking time:** 10 minutes
Servings: 4

Ingredients:

- ➢ 2 chicken breasts, skinless, boneless and cubed
- ➢ 1 red onion, chop
- ➢ 1 red bell pepper, sliced
- ➢ 1/2 cup Italian seasoning
- ➢ 1/2 tsp thyme, dried
- ➢ 2 cups butter lettuce, torn
- ➢ 4 pita pockets
- ➢ 1 cup cherry tomatoes, halved
- ➢ 1 tbsp olive oil

Directions:

1. Toss the chicken with the onion, bell pepper, Italian seasoning, and oil in your air fryer and cook for 10 minutes at 380 degrees F.
2. Transfer the chicken mixture to a bowl, sprinkle in the thyme, butter lettuce, and cherry tomatoes, and serve in pita pockets for lunch. Enjoy!

Nutrition: 126 calories, 4 grams of fat, 8 grams of fiber, 14 grams of carbohydrate, and 4 grams of protein

Fresh Chicken Mix

Preparation time: 10 minutes **Cooking time:** 22 minutes
Servings: 4

Ingredients:

- ➤ 2 chicken breasts, skinless, boneless and cubed
- ➤ 8 button mushrooms, sliced
- ➤ 1 red bell pepper, chop
- ➤ 1 tbsp olive oil
- ➤ 1/2 tsp thyme, dried
- ➤ 10 oz alfredo sauce
- ➤ 6 bread slices
- ➤ 2 tbsp butter, soft

Directions:

1. Combine the chicken, mushrooms, bell pepper, and oil in your air fryer, stir to coat well, and cook for 15 minutes at 350 degrees F.
2. Return the chicken mixture to the air fryer, toss in the thyme and alfredo sauce, and cook for another 4 minutes at 350 degrees F.
3. Spread butter on the bread slices, place them butter side up in the fryer, and cook for another 4 minutes.
4. Serve for lunch by arranging toasted bread slices on a dish and topping each with chicken mixture. Enjoy!

Nutrition: 172 calories, 4 grams of fat, 9 grams of fiber, 12 grams of carbohydrates, and 4 grams of protein

Hot Bacon Sandwiches

Preparation time: 10 minutes **Cooking time:** 7 minutes
Servings: 4

Ingredients:

- ➤ 1/3 cup bbq sauce

- ➢ 2 tbsp honey
- ➢ 8 bacon slices, cooked and cut into thirds
- ➢ 1 red bell pepper, sliced
- ➢ 1 yellow bell pepper, sliced
- ➢ 3 pita pockets, halved
- ➢ 1 and 1/4 cup butter lettuce leaves, torn
- ➢ 2 tomatoes, sliced

Directions:

1. Whisk together the barbecue sauce and honey in a mixing basin.
2. Brush the bacon and all of the bell peppers with some of this mixture, then place them in your air fryer and cook for 4 minutes at 350 degrees F.
3. Cook for another 2 minutes after shaking the fryer.
4. Fill pita pockets with bacon mixture, tomatoes, and lettuce, then top with the remaining bbq sauce and serve for lunch. Enjoy!

Nutrition: 186 calories, 6 grams of fat, 9 grams of fiber, 14 grams of carbohydrates, and 4 grams of protein

Buttermilk Chicken

Preparation time: 10 minutes **Cooking time:** 18 minutes
Servings: 4

Ingredients:

- ➢ 1 and 1/2 pounds chicken thighs
- ➢ 2 cups buttermilk
- ➢ Salt and black pepper to the taste

- ➢ A pinch of cayenne pepper
- ➢ 2 cups white flour
- ➢ 1 tbsp baking powder
- ➢ 1 tbsp sweet paprika
- ➢ 1 tbsp garlic powder

Directions:

1. Toss chicken thighs with buttermilk, salt, pepper, and cayenne in a mixing dish and set aside for 6 hours.
2. In a separate bowl, whisk together flour, paprika, baking powder, and garlic powder.
3. Drain the chicken thighs, dredge them in flour, place them in your air fryer, and cook for 8 minutes at 360 degrees F.
4. Cook for another 10 minutes on the other side, then place on a dish and serve for lunch. Enjoy!

Nutrition: 200 calories, 3 grams of fat, 9 grams of fiber, 14 grams of carbohydrates, and 4 grams of protein

Chicken Pie

Preparation time: 10 minutes **Cooking time:** 16 minutes
Servings: 4

Ingredients:

- ➢ 2 chicken thighs, boneless, skinless and cubed
- ➢ 1 carrot, chop
- ➢ 1 yellow onion, chop
- ➢ 2 potatoes, chop
- ➢ 2 mushrooms, chop
- ➢ 1 tsp soy sauce

- ➢ Salt and black pepper to the taste
- ➢ 1 tsp Italian seasoning
- ➢ 1/2 tsp garlic powder
- ➢ 1 tsp Worcestershire sauce
- ➢ 1 tbsp flour
- ➢ 1 tbsp milk
- ➢ 2 puff pastry sheets
- ➢ 1 tbsp butter, melted

Directions:

1. Heat a pan over medium high heat, add the potatoes, carrots, and onion, and cook for 2 minutes, stirring occasionally.
2. Stir in the chicken and mushrooms, as well as the salt, soy sauce, pepper, Italian seasoning, garlic powder, Worcestershire sauce, flour, and milk. Remove from the heat.
3. Trim the excess puff pastry sheet from the bottom of your air fryer's pan.
4. Add the chicken mixture, then top with the remaining puff pastry sheet, trimming any excess and brushing the pie with butter.
5. Place in your air fryer and cook for 6 minutes at 360 degrees F.
6. Allow the pie to cool before slicing and serving for breakfast. Enjoy!

Nutrition: 300 calories, 5 grams of fat, 7 grams of fiber, 14 grams of carbohydrates, and 7 grams of protein

Macaroni and Cheese

Preparation time: 10 minutes **Cooking time:** 30 minutes
Servings: 3

Ingredients:

- ➢ 1 and 1/2 cups favorite macaroni
- ➢ Cooking spray
- ➢ 1/2 cup heavy cream
- ➢ 1 cup chicken stock
- ➢ 3/4 cup cheddar cheese, shredded
- ➢ 1/2 cup mozzarella cheese, shredded
- ➢ 1/4 cup parmesan, shredded
- ➢ Salt and black pepper to the taste

Directions:

1. Spray a skillet with cooking spray, then add the macaroni, heavy cream, stock, cheddar cheese, mozzarella, and parmesan cheese, as well as salt and pepper, combine well, and cook for 30 minutes in your air fryer's basket.
2. Serve for lunch by dividing the mixture among plates. Enjoy!

Nutrition: 341 calories, 7 grams of fat, 8 grams of fiber, 18 grams of carbohydrates, and 4 grams of protein

Lunch Fajitas

Preparation time: 10 minutes **Cooking time:** 10 minutes
Servings: 4

Ingredients:

- ➢ 1 tsp garlic powder

- ➢ 1/4 tsp cumin, ground
- ➢ 1/2 tsp chili powder
- ➢ Salt and black pepper to the taste
- ➢ 1/4 tsp coriander, ground
- ➢ 1 pound chicken breasts, cut into strips
- ➢ 1 red bell pepper, sliced
- ➢ 1 green bell pepper, sliced
- ➢ 1 yellow onion, chop
- ➢ 1 tbsp lime juice
- ➢ Cooking spray
- ➢ 4 tortillas, warmed up
- ➢ Salsa for serving
- ➢ Sour cream for serving
- ➢ 1 cup lettuce leaves, torn for serving

Directions:

1. Toss chicken with garlic powder, cumin, chile, salt, pepper, coriander, lime juice, red bell pepper, green bell pepper, and onion in a mixing bowl, set aside for 10 minutes, then transfer to an air fryer and spray with cooking spray.
2. Toss and bake for 10 minutes at 400 degrees F.
3. Place tortillas on a work surface, divide the chicken mixture, and top with salsa, sour cream, and lettuce. Wrap and serve for lunch. Enjoy!

Nutrition: 317 calories, 6 grams of fat, 8 grams of fiber, 14 grams of carbohydrates, and 4 grams of protein

Lunch Chicken Salad

Preparation time: 10 minutes **Cooking time:** 20 minutes
Servings: 4

Ingredients:

- 2 ears of corn, hulled
- 1 pound chicken tenders, boneless
- Olive oil as needed
- Salt and black pepper to the taste
- 1 tsp sweet paprika
- 1 tbsp brown sugar
- 1/2 tsp garlic powder
- 1/2 iceberg lettuce head, cut into medium strips
- 1/2 romaine lettuce head, cut into medium strips
- 1 cup canned black beans, drained
- 1 cup cheddar cheese, shredded
- 3 tbsp cilantro, chop
- 4 green onions, chop
- 12 cherry tomatoes, sliced
- 1/4 cup ranch dressing
- 3 tbsp BBQ sauce

Directions:

1. Place the corn in the air fryer, pour with oil, mix, and cook for 10 minutes at 400 degrees F. Transfer to a platter and set aside for now.
2. Put the chicken in the basket of the air fryer, season with salt, pepper, brown sugar, paprika, and garlic powder, stir, sprinkle with extra oil, and cook for 10 minutes at 400 degrees F, flipping halfway through. Transfer the tenders to a cutting board and chop.

3. Remove the corn kernels from the cob and place them in a bowl with the chicken, iceberg lettuce, romaine lettuce, black beans, cheese, cilantro, tomatoes, onions, bbq sauce, and ranch dressing. Toss well to combine and serve for lunch. Enjoy!

Nutrition: 372 calories, 6 grams of fat, 9 grams of fiber, 17 grams of carbohydrates, and 6 grams of protein

Fish And Chips

Preparation time: 10 minutes **Cooking time:** 12 minutes
Servings: 2

Ingredients:

- ➢ 2 medium cod fillets, skinless and boneless
- ➢ Salt and black pepper to the taste
- ➢ 1/4 cup buttermilk
- ➢ 3 cups kettle chips, cooked

Directions:

1. Toss the fish with the salt, pepper, and buttermilk in a basin and set aside for 5 minutes.
2. In a food processor, smash the chips and lay them out on a platter.
3. Add the fish and firmly press it on all sides.
4. Place the fish in the basket of your air fryer and cook for 12 minutes at 400 degrees F.
5. Lunch should be served hot. Enjoy!

Nutrition: 271 calories, 7 grams of fat, 9 grams of fiber, 14 grams of carbohydrates, and 4 grams of protein

Hash Brown Toasts

Preparation time: 10 minutes **Cooking time:** 7 minutes
Servings: 4

Ingredients:

- ➤ 4 hash brown patties, frozen
- ➤ 1 tbsp olive oil
- ➤ 1/4 cup cherry tomatoes, chop
- ➤ 3 tbsp mozzarella, shredded
- ➤ 2 tbsp parmesan, grated
- ➤ 1 tbsp balsamic vinegar
- ➤ 1 tbsp basil, chop

Directions:

1. Place the hash brown patties in your air fryer, pour with oil, and cook for 7 minutes at 400 degrees F.
2. Toss tomatoes with mozzarella, parmesan, vinegar, and basil in a mixing bowl.
3. Serve for lunch by dividing hash brown patties among plates and topping each with tomato mixture. Enjoy!

Nutrition: 199 calories, 3 grams of fat, 8 grams of fiber, 12 grams of carbohydrates, and 4 grams of protein

Delicious Beef Cubes

Preparation time: 10 minutes **Cooking time:** 12 minutes
Servings: 4

Ingredients:

- ➢ 1 pound sirloin, cubed
- ➢ 16 oz jarred pasta sauce
- ➢ 1 and 1/2 cups bread crumbs
- ➢ 2 tbsp olive oil
- ➢ 1/2 tsp marjoram, dried
- ➢ White rice, already cooked for serving

Directions:

1. Toss beef chunks with pasta sauce in a mixing basin.
2. Combine bread crumbs, marjoram, and oil in a separate bowl and toss well.
3. Cook beef cubes in your air fryer at 360 degrees F for 12 minutes after dipping them in this mixture.
4. Serve with white rice on the side and divide among plates. Enjoy!

Nutrition: 271 calories, 6 grams of fat, 9 grams of fiber, 18 grams of carbohydrates, and 12 grams of protein

Pasta Salad

Preparation time: 10 minutes **Cooking time:** 12 minutes
Servings: 6

Ingredients:

- ➢ 1 zucchini, sliced in half and roughly chop
- ➢ 1 orange bell pepper, roughly chop
- ➢ 1 green bell pepper, roughly chop
- ➢ 1 red onion, roughly chop
- ➢ 4 oz brown mushrooms, halved
- ➢ Salt and black pepper to the taste

- ➢ 1 tsp Italian seasoning
- ➢ 1 pound penne rigate, already cooked
- ➢ 1 cup cherry tomatoes, halved
- ➢ 1/2 cup kalamata olive, pitted and halved
- ➢ 1/4 cup olive oil
- ➢ 3 tbsp balsamic vinegar
- ➢ 2 tbsp basil, chop

Directions:

1. Combine zucchini, mushrooms, orange bell pepper, green bell pepper, red onion, salt, pepper, Italian seasoning, and oil in a mixing bowl, combine well, and cook for 12 minutes in a prepared air fryer at 380 degrees F.
2. Toss spaghetti with cooked vegetables, cherry tomatoes, olives, vinegar, and basil in a big salad bowl, toss, and serve for lunch. Enjoy!

Nutrition: 200 calories, 5 grams of fat, 8 grams of fiber, 10 grams of carbohydrates, and 6 grams of protein

Potato Wedges

Preparation time: 10 minutes **Cooking time:** 25 minutes
Servings: 4

Ingredients:

- ➢ 2 potatoes, cut into wedges
- ➢ 1 tbsp olive oil
- ➢ Salt and black pepper to the taste
- ➢ 3 tbsp sour cream
- ➢ 2 tbsp sweet chili sauce

Directions:

1. Toss potato wedges with oil, salt, and pepper in a mixing basin, then transfer to an air fryer basket and cook for 25 minutes, flipping once.
2. Serve potato wedges as a side dish by dividing them among plates and drizzling sour cream and chili sauce over them. Enjoy!

Nutrition: 171 calories, 8 grams of fat, 9 grams of fiber, 18 grams of carbohydrates, and 7 grams of protein

Mushroom Side Dish

Preparation time: 10 minutes **Cooking time:** 8 minutes
Servings: 4

Ingredients:

- ➢ 10 button mushrooms, stems removed
- ➢ 1 tbsp Italian seasoning
- ➢ Salt and black pepper to the taste
- ➢ 2 tbsp cheddar cheese, grated
- ➢ 1 tbsp olive oil
- ➢ 2 tbsp mozzarella, grated
- ➢ 1 tbsp dill, chop

Directions:

1. Mix mushrooms, Italian seasoning, salt, pepper, oil, and dill in a bowl and rub well.
2. Place the mushrooms in the air fryer basket, top with mozzarella and cheddar, and cook for 8 minutes at 360

degrees F.

3. Serve as a side dish by dividing them among plates. Enjoy!

Nutrition: 241 calories, 7 grams of fat, 8 grams of fiber, 14 grams of carbohydrates, and 6 grams of protein

Sweet Potato Fries

Preparation time: 10 minutes **Cooking time:** 20 minutes
Servings: 2

Ingredients:

➤ 2 sweet potatoes, peeled and cut into medium fries
➤ Salt and black pepper to the taste
➤ 2 tbsp olive oil
➤ 1/2 tsp curry powder
➤ 1/4 tsp coriander, ground
➤ 1/4 cup ketchup
➤ 2 tbsp mayonnaise
➤ 1/2 tsp cumin, ground
➤ A pinch of ginger powder
➤ A pinch of cinnamon powder

Directions:

1. Mix sweet potato fries with salt, pepper, coriander, curry powder, and oil in the basket of your air fryer, toss well, and cook at 370 degrees F for 20 minutes, flipping once.
2. Meanwhile, stir together ketchup, mayonnaise, cumin, ginger, and cinnamon in a mixing dish.

3. Serve as a side dish by dividing the fries among plates and drizzling the ketchup mixture over them. Enjoy!

Nutrition: 200 calories, 5 grams of fat, 8 grams of fiber, 9 grams of carbohydrates, and 7 grams of protein

Corn with Lime and Cheese

Preparation time: 10 minutes **Cooking time:** 15 minutes
Servings: 2

Ingredients:

- ➢ 2 corns on the cob, husks removed
- ➢ A drizzle of olive oil
- ➢ 1/2 cup feta cheese, grated
- ➢ 2 tsp sweet paprika
- ➢ Juice from 2 limes

Directions:

1. Corn should be rubbed with oil and paprika, placed in an air fryer, and cooked for 15 minutes at 400 degrees F, flipping once.
2. Divide the corn amongst plates, cover with cheese, drizzle with lime juice, and serve as a side dish. Enjoy!

Nutrition: 200 calories, 5 grams of fat, 2 grams of fiber, 6 grams of carbohydrates, and 6 grams of protein

Hassel back Potatoes

Preparation time: 10 minutes **Cooking time:** 20 minutes
Servings: 2

Ingredients:

- ➤ 2 potatoes, peeled and thinly sliced almost all the way horizontally
- ➤ 2 tbsp olive oil
- ➤ 1 tsp garlic, minced
- ➤ Salt and black pepper to the taste
- ➤ 1/2 tsp oregano, dried
- ➤ 1/2 tsp basil, dried
- ➤ 1/2 tsp sweet paprika

Directions:

1. Whisk together the oil, garlic, salt, pepper, oregano, basil, and paprika in a bowl.
2. Rub the potatoes with this mixture, then place them in the basket of your air fryer and cook for 20 minutes at 360 degrees F.
3. Serve as a side dish by dividing them among plates. Enjoy!

Nutrition: 172 calories, 6 grams of fat, 6 grams of fiber, 9 grams of carbohydrates, and 6 grams of protein

Brussels Sprouts Side Dish

Preparation time: 10 minutes **Cooking time:** 15 minutes
Servings: 4

Ingredients:

- ➤ 1 pound Brussels sprouts, trimmed and halved
- ➤ Salt and black pepper to the taste
- ➤ 6 tsp olive oil
- ➤ 1/2 tsp thyme, chop
- ➤ 1/2 cup mayonnaise
- ➤ 2 tbsp roasted garlic, crushed

Directions:

1. Combine Brussels sprouts, salt, pepper, and oil in an air fryer, toss well, and cook for 15 minutes at 390 degrees F.
2. Meanwhile, whisk together the thyme, mayonnaise, and garlic in a mixing dish.
3. Serve Brussels sprouts as a side dish by dividing them among plates and drizzling them with garlic sauce. Enjoy!

Nutrition: 172 calories, 6 grams of fat, 8 grams of fiber, 12 grams of carbohydrates, and 6 grams of protein

Creamy Air Fried Potato Side Dish

Preparation time: 10 minutes **Cooking time:** 1 hour and 20 minutes **Servings: 2**

Ingredients:

- ➤ 1 big potato
- ➤ 2 bacon strips, cooked and chop
- ➤ 1 tsp olive oil
- ➤ 1/3 cup cheddar cheese, shredded
- ➤ 1 tbsp green onions, chop
- ➤ Salt and black pepper to the taste

➢ 1 tbsp butter
➢ 2 tbsp heavy cream

Directions:

1. Rub potato with oil, season with salt and pepper, then cook for 30 minutes at 400 degrees F in a preheated air fryer.
2. Cook for another 30 minutes on the other side, then move to a chopping board, cool, slice in half lengthwise, and scrape pulp into a bowl.
3. Stir in the bacon, cheese, butter, heavy cream, green onions, salt, and pepper before stuffing the potato skins.
4. Return the potatoes to the air fryer and cook for 20 minutes at 400 degrees F.
5. Serve as a side dish by dividing the mixture among plates. Enjoy!

Nutrition: 172 calories, 5 grams of fat, 7 grams of fiber, 9 grams of carbohydrates, and 4 grams of protein

Green Beans Side Dish

Preparation time: 10 minutes **Cooking time:** 25 minutes
Servings: 4

Ingredients:

➢1 and 1/2 pounds green beans, trimmed and steamed for 2 minutes
➢ Salt and black pepper to the taste
➢ 1/2 pound shallots, chop
➢ 1/4 cup almonds, toasted

➢ 2 tbsp olive oil

Directions:

1. Toss green beans with salt, pepper, shallots, almonds, and oil in the basket of your air fryer, toss well, and cook at 400 degrees F for 25 minutes.
2. Serve as a side dish by dividing the mixture among plates. Enjoy!

Nutrition: 152 calories, 3 grams of fat, 6 grams of fiber, 7 grams of carbohydrates, and 4 grams of protein

Roasted Pumpkin

Preparation time: 10 minutes **Cooking time:** 12 minutes
Servings: 4

Ingredients:

➢1 and 1/2 pound pumpkin, deseeded, sliced and roughly chop
➢ 3 garlic cloves, minced
➢ 1 tbsp olive oil
➢ A pinch of sea salt
➢ A pinch of brown sugar
➢ A pinch of nutmeg, ground
➢ A pinch of cinnamon powder

Directions:

1. Combine pumpkin, garlic, oil, salt, brown sugar, cinnamon, and nutmeg in the basket of your air fryer, toss well, cover, and cook at 370 degrees F for 12 minutes.

2. Serve as a side dish by dividing the mixture among plates. Enjoy!

Nutrition: 200 calories, 5 grams of fat, 4 grams of fiber, 7 grams of carbohydrates, and 4 grams of protein

Parmesan Mushrooms

Preparation time: 10 minutes **Cooking time:** 15 minutes **Servings:** 3

Ingredients:

- ➢ 9 button mushroom caps
- ➢ 3 cream cracker slices, crumbled
- ➢ 1 egg white
- ➢ 2 tbsp parmesan, grated
- ➢ 1 tsp Italian seasoning
- ➢ A pinch of salt and black pepper
- ➢ 1 tbsp butter, melted

Directions:

1. Mix crackers, egg white, parmesan, Italian seasoning, butter, salt, and pepper in a mixing bowl until well combined, then stuff mushrooms with the mixture.
2. Place the mushrooms in the basket of your air fryer and cook for 15 minutes at 360°F.
3. Serve as a side dish by dividing among plates. Enjoy!

Nutrition: 124 calories, 4 grams of fat, 4 grams of fiber, 7 grams of carbohydrates, and 3 grams of protein

Garlic Potatoes

Preparation time: 10 minutes **Cooking time:** 20 minutes
Servings: 6

Ingredients:

- ➤ 2 tbsp parsley, chop
- ➤ 5 garlic cloves, minced
- ➤ 1/2 tsp basil, dried
- ➤ 1/2 tsp oregano, dried
- ➤ 3 pounds red potatoes, halved
- ➤ 1 tsp thyme, dried
- ➤ 2 tbsp olive oil
- ➤ Salt and black pepper to the taste
- ➤ 2 tbsp butter
- ➤ 1/3 cup parmesan, grated

Directions:

1. Toss potato halves with parsley, garlic, basil, oregano, thyme, salt, pepper, oil, and butter in a bowl until well combined, then move to the basket of the air fryer.
2. Cover and bake for 20 minutes at 400 degrees F, flipping once.
3. Serve as a side dish by sprinkling parmesan cheese on top and dividing the potatoes among plates. Enjoy!

Nutrition: 162 calories, 5 grams of fat, 5 grams of fiber, 7 grams of carbohydrates, 5 grams of protein

Eggplant Side Dish

Preparation time: 10 minutes **Cooking time:** 10 minutes
Servings: 4

Ingredients:

- ➤ 8 baby eggplants, scooped in the center and pulp reserved
- ➤ Salt and black pepper to the taste
- ➤ A pinch of oregano, dried
- ➤ 1 green bell pepper, chop
- ➤ 1 tbsp tomato paste
- ➤ 1 bunch coriander, chop
- ➤ 1/2 tsp garlic powder
- ➤ 1 tbsp olive oil
- ➤ 1 yellow onion, chop
- ➤ 1 tomato chop

Directions:

1. Heat the oil in a skillet over medium heat, then add the onion, swirl, and cook for 1 minute.
2. Season with salt and pepper, then whisk in the eggplant pulp, oregano, green bell pepper, tomato paste, garlic powder, coriander, and tomato. Cook for another 1-2 minutes, then remove from heat and cool.
3. Fill eggplants with the mixture, lay them in the basket of your air fryer, and cook for 8 minutes at 360 degrees F.
4. Serve the eggplants as a side dish, divided among plates. Enjoy!

Nutrition: 200 calories, 3 grams of fat, 7 grams of fiber, 12 grams of carbohydrates, and 4 grams of protein

Mushrooms and Sour Cream

Preparation time: 10 minutes **Cooking time:** 10 minutes
Servings: 6

Ingredients:

- ➢ 2 bacon strips, chop
- ➢ 1 yellow onion, chop
- ➢ 1 green bell pepper, chop
- ➢ 24 mushrooms, stems removed
- ➢ 1 carrot, grated
- ➢ 1/2 cup sour cream
- ➢ 1 cup cheddar cheese, grated
- ➢ Salt and black pepper to the taste

Directions:

1. Heat a skillet over medium-high heat, then add the bacon, onion, bell pepper, and carrot, stirring constantly for 1 minute.
2. Stir in the salt, pepper, and sour cream, cook for another minute, then remove from heat and cool.
3. Stuff mushrooms with the mixture, top with cheese, and bake for 8 minutes at 360 degrees F.
4. Serve as a side dish by dividing the mixture among plates. Enjoy!

Nutrition: 211 calories, 4 grams of fat, 7 grams of fiber, 8 grams of carbohydrates, and 3 grams of protein

Fried Tomatoes

Preparation time: 10 minutes **Cooking time:** 5 minutes
Servings: 4

Ingredients:

- ➢ 2 green tomatoes, sliced
- ➢ Salt and black pepper to the taste
- ➢ 1/2 cup flour
- ➢ 1 cup buttermilk
- ➢ 1 cup panko bread crumbs
- ➢ 1/2 tbsp Creole seasoning
- ➢ Cooking spray

Directions:

1. Sprinkle salt and pepper on tomato slices.
2. In a large mixing bowl, combine flour, buttermilk, and panko crumbs with Creole spice.
3. Dredge tomato slices in flour, buttermilk, and panko bread crumbs, then set them in an oiled air fryer basket for 5 minutes at 400 degrees F.
4. Serve as a side dish by dividing among plates. Enjoy!

Nutrition: 124 calories, 5 grams of fat, 7 grams of fiber, 9 grams of carbohydrates, and 4 grams of protein

Cauliflower Cakes

Preparation time: 10 minutes **Cooking time:** 10 minutes
Servings: 6

Ingredients:

- ➢ 3 and 1/2 cups cauliflower rice
- ➢ 2 eggs
- ➢ 1/4 cup white flour

- ➤ 1/2 cup parmesan, grated
- ➤ Salt and black pepper to the taste
- ➤ Cooking spray

Directions:

1. Combine the cauliflower rice, salt, and pepper in a mixing bowl, stirring to combine. Squeeze off any excess water.
2. Transfer the cauliflower to a separate bowl, along with the eggs, salt, pepper, flour, and parmesan cheese, and combine thoroughly before forming your cakes.
3. Spray your air fryer with cooking spray, preheat to 400°F, then add the cauliflower cakes and cook for 10 minutes, flipping halfway through.
4. As a side dish, divide the cakes among plates and serve. Enjoy!

Nutrition: 125 calories, 2 grams of fat, 6 grams of fiber, 8 grams of carbohydrates, 3 grams of protein

Cheddar Biscuits

Preparation time: 10 minutes **Cooking time:** 20 minutes
Servings: 8

Ingredients:

- ➤ 2 and 1/3 cup self-rising flour
- ➤ 1/2 cup butter+ 1 tbsp, melted
- ➤ 2 tbsp sugar
- ➤ 1/2 cup cheddar cheese, grated
- ➤ 1 and 1/3 cup buttermilk
- ➤ 1 cup flour

Directions:

1. Combine self-rising flour, 1/2 cup butter, sugar, cheddar cheese, and buttermilk in a mixing dish and whisk until a dough forms.
2. Spread 1 cup flour on a work area, spread out the dough, flatten it, and cut 8 circles using a cookie cutter.
3. Line the basket of your air fryer with tin foil, add the biscuits, coat them with melted butter, and bake for 20 minutes at 380 degrees F.
4. Serve as a side dish by dividing the mixture among plates. Enjoy!

Nutrition: 221 calories, 3 grams of fat, 8 grams of fiber, 12 grams of carbohydrates, and 4 grams of protein

Zucchini Fries

Preparation time: 10 minutes **Cooking time:** 12 minutes
Servings: 4

Ingredients:

- 1 zucchini, cut into medium sticks
- A drizzle of olive oil
- Salt and black pepper to the taste
- 2 eggs, whisked
- 1 cup bread crumbs
- 1/2 cup flour

Directions:

1. In a mixing bowl, combine flour, salt, and pepper, and toss to combine.
2. Place breadcrumbs in a separate bowl.
3. In a third bowl, whisk together eggs and season with salt and pepper.
4. Dredge the zucchini fries in flour, then in eggs, and last in bread crumbs.
5. Cook zucchini fries for 12 minutes in an air fryer greased with olive oil and heated to 400 degrees F.
6. As a side dish, serve them. Enjoy!

Nutrition: 172 calories, 3 grams of fat, 3 grams of fiber, 7 grams of carbohydrates, 3 grams of protein

Herbed Tomatoes

Preparation time: 10 minutes **Cooking time:** 15 minutes
Servings: 4

Ingredients:

➢ 4 big tomatoes, halved and insides scooped out
➢ Salt and black pepper to the taste
➢ 1 tbsp olive oil
➢ 2 garlic cloves, minced
➢ 1/2 tsp thyme, chop

Directions:

1. Toss tomatoes with salt, pepper, oil, garlic, and thyme in your air fryer and cook for 15 minutes at 390 degrees F.
2. Serve as a side dish by dividing the mixture among plates. Enjoy!

Nutrition: 112 calories, 1 gram fat, 3 gram fiber, 4 gram carbohydrates, 4 gram protein

Roasted Peppers

Preparation time: 10 minutes **Cooking time:** 20 minutes **Servings:** 4

Ingredients:

- ➢ 1 tbsp sweet paprika
- ➢ 1 tbsp olive oil
- ➢ 4 red bell peppers, cut into medium strips
- ➢ 4 green bell peppers, cut into medium strips
- ➢ 4 yellow bell peppers, cut into medium strips
- ➢ 1 yellow onion, chop
- ➢ Salt and black pepper to the taste

Directions:

1. Combine red, green, and yellow bell peppers in your air fryer.
2. Toss in the paprika, oil, onion, salt, and pepper, and bake for 20 minutes at 350 degrees F.
3. Serve as a side dish by dividing the mixture among plates. Enjoy!

Nutrition: 142 calories, 4 grams of fat, 4 grams of fiber, 7 grams of carbohydrates, and 4 grams of protein

Delicious Roasted Carrots

Preparation time: 10 minutes **Cooking time:** 20 minutes
Servings: 4

Ingredients:

- ➢ 1 pound baby carrots
- ➢ 2 tsp olive oil
- ➢ 1 tsp herbs de Provence
- ➢ 4 tbsp orange juice

Directions:

1. Toss carrots with herbs de Provence, oil, and orange juice in the basket of your air fryer and cook for 20 minutes at 320 degrees F.
2. Serve as a side dish by dividing the mixture among plates. Enjoy!

Nutrition: 112 calories, 2 grams of fat, 3 grams of fiber, 4 grams of carbohydrates, 3 grams of protein

Vermouth Mushrooms

Preparation time: 10 minutes **Cooking time:** 25 minutes
Servings: 4

Ingredients:

- ➢ 1 tbsp olive oil
- ➢ 2 pounds white mushrooms
- ➢ 2 tbsp white vermouth
- ➢ 2 tsp herbs de Provence
- ➢ 2 garlic cloves, minced

Directions:

1. Mix oil with mushrooms, herbs de Provence, and garlic in your air fryer, toss, and cook at 350 degrees F for 20 minutes.
2. Toss in the vermouth and simmer for another 5 minutes.
3. Serve as a side dish by dividing the mixture among plates. Enjoy!

Nutrition: 121 calories, 2 grams of fat, 5 grams of fiber, 7 grams of carbohydrates, and 4 grams of protein

Roasted Parsnips

Preparation time: 10 minutes **Cooking time:** 40 minutes
Servings: 6

Ingredients:

- ➢ 2 pounds parsnips, peeled and cut into medium chunks
- ➢ 2 tbsp maple syrup
- ➢ 1 tbsp parsley flakes, dried
- ➢ 1 tbsp olive oil

Directions:

1. Preheat your air fryer to 360°F, then add the oil and heat it up.
2. Toss in the parsnips, parsley flakes, and maple syrup before cooking for 40 minutes.
3. Serve as a side dish by dividing the mixture among plates. Enjoy!

Nutrition: 124 calories, 3 grams of fat, 3 grams of fiber, 7 grams of carbohydrates, 4 grams of protein

Barley Risotto

Preparation time: 10 minutes **Cooking time:** 30 minutes
Servings: 8

Ingredients:

- ➤ 5 cups veggie stock
- ➤ 3 tbsp olive oil
- ➤ 2 yellow onions, chop
- ➤ 2 garlic cloves, minced
- ➤ 3/4 pound barley
- ➤ 3 oz mushrooms, sliced
- ➤ 2 oz skim milk
- ➤ 1 tsp thyme, dried
- ➤ 1 tsp tarragon, dried
- ➤ Salt and black pepper to the taste
- ➤ 2 pounds sweet potato, peeled and chop

Directions:

1. In a pot, combine the stock and barley, mix to combine, and bring to a boil over medium heat. Cook for 15 minutes.
2. Preheat your air fryer to 350 degrees F, then add the oil and heat again.
3. Cook for another 15 minutes after adding the barley, onions, garlic, mushrooms, milk, salt, pepper, tarragon, and sweet potato.

4. Serve as a side dish by dividing the mixture among plates. Enjoy!

Nutrition: 124 calories, 4 grams of fat, 4 grams of fiber, 6 grams of carbohydrates, and 4 grams of protein

Coconut Chicken Bites

Preparation time: 10 minutes **Cooking time:** 13 minutes
Servings: 4

Ingredients:

- ➤ 2 tsp garlic powder
- ➤ 2 eggs
- ➤ Salt and black pepper to the taste
- ➤ 3/4 cup panko bread crumbs
- ➤ 3/4 cup coconut, shredded
- ➤ Cooking spray
- ➤ 8 chicken tenders

Directions:

1. Whisk together eggs, salt, pepper, and garlic powder in a mixing bowl.
2. In a separate bowl, combine the coconut and panko and whisk thoroughly.
3. Chicken tenders are dipped in an egg mixture and then well coated in coconut.
4. Spray the chicken bites with cooking spray, set them in the air fryer basket, and cook for 10 minutes at 350 degrees F.
5. Serve as an appetizer by arranging them on a dish. Enjoy!

Nutrition: 252 calories, 4 grams of fat, 2 grams of fiber, 14 grams of carbohydrates, and 24 grams of protein

Buffalo Cauliflower Snack

Preparation time: 10 minutes **Cooking time:** 15 minutes
Servings: 4

Ingredients:

- 4 cups cauliflower florets
- 1 cup panko bread crumbs
- 1/4 cup butter, melted
- 1/4 cup buffalo sauce
- Mayonnaise for serving

Directions:

1. Buffalo sauce and butter should be whisked together in a bowl.
2. Cauliflower florets are coated in panko bread crumbs after being dipped in this mixture.
3. Cook for 15 minutes at 350 degrees F in the basket of your air fryer.
4. Serve with mayonnaise on the side. Enjoy!

Nutrition: 241 calories, 4 grams of fat, 7 grams of fiber, 8 grams of carbohydrates, and 4 grams of protein

Banana Snack

Preparation time: 10 minutes **Cooking time:** 5 minutes
Servings: 8

Ingredients:

- ➤ 16 baking cups crust
- ➤ 1/4 cup peanut butter
- ➤ 3/4 cup chocolate chips
- ➤ 1 banana, peeled and sliced into 16 pieces
- ➤ 1 tbsp vegetable oil

Directions:

1. In a small pot, melt chocolate chips over low heat, stirring constantly until completely melted. Remove from heat.
2. Whisk together peanut butter and coconut oil in a mixing basin.
3. In a cup, put 1 tsp chocolate mix, 1 banana slice, and 1 tsp butter mix on top.
4. Repeat with the remaining cups, placing them all in a dish that fits your air fryer, cooking for 5 minutes at 320 degrees F, then transferring to a freezer and keeping them there until ready to serve as a snack. Enjoy!

Nutrition: 70 calories, 4 grams of fat, 1 gram of fiber, 10 grams of carbohydrates, 1 gram of protein

Potato Spread

Preparation time: 10 minutes **Cooking time:** 10 minutes
Servings: 10

Ingredients:

- ➢ 19 oz canned garbanzo beans, drained
- ➢ 1 cup sweet potatoes, peeled and chop
- ➢ 1/4 cup tahini
- ➢ 2 tbsp lemon juice
- ➢ 1 tbsp olive oil
- ➢ 5 garlic cloves, minced
- ➢ 1/2 tsp cumin, ground
- ➢ 2 tbsp water
- ➢ A pinch of salt and white pepper

Directions:

1. Place potatoes in the basket of your air fryer and cook for 15 minutes at 360 degrees F. Cool, peel, and grind in a food processor. basket,
2. Pulse the sesame paste, garlic, beans, lemon juice, cumin, water, and oil until smooth.
3. Season with salt and pepper, pulse one more, then divide into bowls and serve. Enjoy!

Nutrition: 200 calories, 3 grams of fat, 10 grams of fiber, 20 grams of carbohydrates, 11 grams of protein

Mexican Apple Snack

Preparation time: 10 minutes **Cooking time:** 5 minutes
Servings: 4

Ingredients:

- ➢ 3 big apples, cored, peeled and cubed
- ➢ 2 tsp lemon juice
- ➢ 1/4 cup pecans, chop

- ➢ 1/2 cup dark chocolate chips
- ➢ 1/2 cup clean caramel sauce

Directions:

1. Combine apples and lemon juice in a mixing dish, whisk well, and transfer to an air fryer pan.
2. Toss in the chocolate chips and pecans with the caramel sauce, then transfer to your air fryer and cook for 5 minutes at 320 degrees F.
3. Gently toss, divide into small bowls, and serve as a snack immediately soon. Enjoy!

Nutrition: 200 calories, 4 grams of fat, 3 grams of fiber, 20 grams of carbohydrates, and 3 grams of protein

Shrimp Muffins

Preparation time: 10 minutes **Cooking time:** 26 minutes
Servings: 6

Ingredients:

- ➢ 1 spaghetti squash, peeled and halved
- ➢ 2 tbsp mayonnaise
- ➢ 1 cup mozzarella, shredded
- ➢ 8 oz shrimp, peeled, cooked and chop
- ➢ 1 and 1/2 cups panko
- ➢ 1 tsp parsley flakes
- ➢ 1 garlic clove, minced
- ➢ Salt and black pepper to the taste
- ➢ Cooking spray

Directions:

1. Cook the squash halves in the air fryer for 16 minutes at 350 degrees F, then set aside to cool and scrape the flesh into a basin.
2. Stir in the salt, pepper, parsley flakes, panko, shrimp, mayo, and mozzarella.
3. Cooking spray a muffin pan that fits your air fryer and distribute the squash and shrimp mixture into each cup.
4. Place in the fryer and cook for 10 minutes at 360 degrees F.
5. Serve muffins as a snack by arranging them on a dish. Enjoy!

Nutrition: 60 calories, 2 grams of fat, 0.4 grams of fiber, 4 grams of carbohydrates, and 4 grams of protein

Zucchini Cakes

Preparation time: 10 minutes **Cooking time:** 12 minutes
Servings: 12

Ingredients:

➤ Cooking spray
➤ 1/2 cup dill, chop
➤ 1 egg
➤ 1/2 cup whole wheat flour
➤ Salt and black pepper to the taste
➤ 1 yellow onion, chop
➤ 2 garlic cloves, minced
➤ 3 zucchinis, grated

Directions:

1. Mix zucchinis with garlic, onion, flour, salt, pepper, egg, and dill in a mixing bowl. Form tiny patties out of this mixture, coat them with cooking spray, and place them in your air fryer's basket. Cook for 6 minutes on each side at 370 degrees F.
2. Serve them as soon as possible as a snack. Enjoy!

Nutrition: 60 calories, 1 gram of fat, 2 gram of fiber, 6 gram of carbohydrates, 2 gram of protein

Cauliflower Bars

Preparation time: 10 minutes **Cooking time:** 25 minutes
Servings: 12

Ingredients:

➢ 1 big cauliflower head, florets separated
➢ 1/2 cup mozzarella, shredded
➢ 1/4 cup egg whites
➢ 1 tsp Italian seasoning
➢ Salt and black pepper to the tast

Directions:

1. Place cauliflower florets in a food processor and pulse until smooth. Spread on a lined baking sheet that fits your air fryer, place in fryer, and cook for 10 minutes at 360 degrees F.
2. Transfer cauliflower to a mixing basin, add salt, pepper, cheese, egg whites, and Italian seasoning, toss well,

spread into a rectangle pan that fits your air fryer, press well, place in fryer, and cook for another 15 minutes at 360 degrees F.

3. Serve as a snack by cutting into 12 bars and arranging them on a dish. Enjoy!

Nutrition: 50 calories, 1 gram of fat, 2 gram of fiber, 3 gram of carbohydrates, 3 gram of protein

Pesto Crackers

Preparation time: 10 minutes **Cooking time:** 17 minutes
Servings: 6

Ingredients:

➤ 1/2 tsp baking powder
➤ Salt and black pepper to the taste
➤ 1 and 1/4 cups flour
➤ 1/4 tsp basil, dried
➤ 1 garlic clove, minced
➤ 2 tbsp basil pesto
➤ 3 tbsp butter

Directions:

1. Combine salt, pepper, baking powder, flour, garlic, cayenne, basil, pesto, and butter in a mixing bowl and whisk until a dough forms.
2. Spread the dough out on a lined baking sheet that will fit in your air fryer, then bake for 17 minutes at 325 degrees F.
3. Allow to cool before cutting into crackers and serving as a snack. Enjoy!

Nutrition: 200 calories, 20 grams of fat, 1 gram of fiber, 4 grams of carbohydrates, and 7 grams of protein

Pumpkin Muffins

Preparation time: 10 minutes **Cooking time:** 15 minutes
Servings: 18

Ingredients:

- 1/4 cup butter
- 3/4 cup pumpkin puree
- 2 tbsp flaxseed meal
- 1/4 cup flour
- 1/2 cup sugar
- 1/2 tsp nutmeg, ground
- 1 tsp cinnamon powder
- 1/2 tsp baking soda
- 1 egg
- 1/2 tsp baking powder

Directions:

1. Combine butter, pumpkin puree, and egg in a mixing dish and well combine.
2. Stir together the flaxseed meal, flour, sugar, baking soda, baking powder, nutmeg, and cinnamon.
3. Fill a muffin tin that fits your fryer with this mixture. Introduce to the fryer and bake for 15 minutes at 350 degrees F.
4. As a snack, serve muffins cold. Enjoy!

Nutrition: 50 calories, 3 grams of fat, 1 gram of fiber, 2 grams of carbohydrate, and 2 grams of protein

Zucchini Chips

Preparation time: 10 minutes **Cooking time:** 1 hour **Servings:** 6

Ingredients:

- ➤ 3 zucchinis, thinly sliced
- ➤ Salt and black pepper to the taste
- ➤ 2 tbsp olive oil
- ➤ 2 tbsp balsamic vinegar

Directions:

1. Whisk together the oil, vinegar, salt, and pepper in a mixing bowl.
2. Toss zucchini slices in a bowl to coat well, then place in your air fryer and cook for 1 hour at 200 degrees F.
3. As a snack, serve zucchini chips chilled. Enjoy!

Nutrition: 40 calories, 3 grams of fat, 7 grams of fiber, 3 grams of carbohydrates, and 7 grams of protein

Beef Jerky Snack

Preparation time: 2 hours **Cooking time:** 1 hour and 30 minutes **Servings:** 6

Ingredients:

- ➤ 2 cups soy sauce

- ➤ 1/2 cup Worcestershire sauce
- ➤ 2 tbsp black peppercorns
- ➤ 2 tbsp black pepper
- ➤ 2 pounds beef round, sliced

Directions:

1. Whisk together the soy sauce, black peppercorns, black pepper, and Worcestershire sauce in a mixing bowl.
2. Add the beef slices, mix to coat, and refrigerate for 6 hours.
3. Place the beef rounds in your air fryer and cook for 1 hour and 30 minutes at 370 degrees F.
4. Transfer to a bowl and chill before serving. Enjoy!

Nutrition: 300 calories, 12 grams of fat, 4 grams of fiber, 3 grams of carbohydrates, and 8 grams of protein

Honey Party Wings

Preparation time: 1 hour and 10 minutes **Cooking time:** 12 minutes **Servings:** 8

Ingredients:

- ➤ 16 chicken wings, halved
- ➤ 2 tbsp soy sauce
- ➤ 2 tbsp honey
- ➤ Salt and black pepper to the taste
- ➤ 2 tbsp lime juice

Directions:

1. Toss chicken wings with soy sauce, honey, salt, pepper, and lime juice in a basin, toss well, and chill for 1 hour.
2. Cook the chicken wings in your air fryer at 360 degrees F for 12 minutes, flipping halfway through.
3. Serve as an appetizer by arranging them on a dish. Enjoy!

Nutrition: 211 calories, 4 grams of fat, 7 grams of fiber, 14 grams of carbohydrate, and 3 grams of protein

Salmon Party Patties

Preparation time: 10 minutes **Cooking time:** 22 minutes
Servings: 4

Ingredients:

- ➢ 3 big potatoes, boiled, drained and mashed
- ➢ 1 big salmon fillet, skinless, boneless
- ➢ 2 tbsp parsley, chop
- ➢ 2 tbsp dill, chop
- ➢ Salt and black pepper to the taste
- ➢ 1 egg
- ➢ 2 tbsp bread crumbs
- ➢ Cooking spray

Directions:

1. Place the salmon in the basket of your air fryer and cook for 10 minutes at 360°F.
2. Cool the salmon on a cutting board before flaking it and placing it in a bowl.
3. Stir in the mashed potatoes, salt, pepper, dill, parsley, egg, and bread crumbs, then form 8 patties from the mixture.

4. Place the salmon patties in the basket of your air fryer, spry them with cooking oil, and cook for 12 minutes at 360 degrees F, flipping halfway through. Transfer to a tray and serve as an appetizer. Enjoy!

Nutrition: 231 calories, 3 grams of fat, 7 grams of fiber, 14 grams of carbohydrates, and 4 grams of protein

Tasty Air Fried Cod

Preparation time: 10 minutes **Cooking time:** 12 minutes
Servings: 4

Ingredients:

- ➢ 2 cod fish, 7 oz each
- ➢ A drizzle of sesame oil
- ➢ Salt and black pepper to the taste
- ➢ 1 cup water
- ➢ 1 tsp dark soy sauce
- ➢ 4 tbsp light soy sauce
- ➢ 1 tbsp sugar
- ➢ 3 tbsp olive oil
- ➢ 4 ginger slices
- ➢ 3 spring onions, chop
- ➢ 2 tbsp coriander, chop

Directions:

1. Season the fish with salt and pepper, then drizzle sesame oil over it and rub it in well. Set aside for 10 minutes.

2. Cook the salmon for 12 minutes at 356 degrees F in your air fryer.
3. Meanwhile, heat the water in a pot over medium heat, then add the dark and light soy sauces and sugar, mix to combine, bring to a simmer, and remove from heat.
4. Heat the olive oil in a pan over medium heat, then add the ginger and green onions, stir, and simmer for a few minutes before turning off the heat.
5. Serve immediately by dividing the fish amongst plates, topping with ginger and green onions, drizzled with soy sauce mixture, and coriander. Enjoy!

Nutrition: 300 calories, 17 grams of fat, 8 grams of fiber, 20 grams of carbohydrates, 22 grams of protein

Delicious Catfish

Preparation time: 10 minutes **Cooking time:** 20 minutes
Servings: 4

Ingredients:

- ➤ 4 cat fish fillets
- ➤ Salt and black pepper to the taste
- ➤ A pinch of sweet paprika
- ➤ 1 tbsp parsley, chop
- ➤ 1 tbsp lemon juice
- ➤ 1 tbsp olive oil

Directions:

1. Season catfish fillets with salt, pepper, and paprika, sprinkle with oil, and rub well before placing in the air fryer

basket and cooking for 20 minutes at 400 degrees F, flipping after 10 minutes.
2. Serve the fish on plates with lemon juice drizzled over it and parsley sprinkled on top. Enjoy!

Nutrition: 253 calories, 6 grams of fat, 12 grams of fiber, 26 grams of carbohydrates, 22 grams of protein

Cod Fillets with Fennel and Grapes Salad

Preparation time: 10 minutes **Cooking time:** 15 minutes
Servings: 2

Ingredients:

- ➤ 2 black cod fillets, boneless
- ➤ 1 tbsp olive oil
- ➤ Salt and black pepper to the taste
- ➤ 1 fennel bulb, thinly sliced
- ➤ 1 cup grapes, halved
- ➤ 1/2 cup pecans

Directions:

1. Drizzle half of the oil over the fish fillets, season with salt and pepper, rub well, place fillets in air fryer basket, and cook for 10 minutes at 400 degrees F.
2. Toss pecans with grapes, fennel, the remainder of the oil, salt, and pepper in a dish to coat, then transfer to a pan that fits your air fryer and cook for 5 minutes at 400 degrees F.
3. Serve the cod on plates with the fennel and grapes mix on the side. Enjoy!

Nutrition: 300 calories, 4 grams of fat, 2 grams of fiber, 32 grams of carbohydrates, 22 grams of protein

Tabasco Shrimp

Preparation time: 10 minutes **Cooking time:** 10 minutes
Servings: 4

Ingredients:

- ➤ 1 pound shrimp, peeled and deveined
- ➤ 1 tsp red pepper flakes
- ➤ 2 tbsp olive oil
- ➤ 1 tsp Tabasco sauce
- ➤ 2 tbsp water
- ➤ 1 tsp oregano, dried
- ➤ Salt and black pepper to the taste
- ➤ 1/2 tsp parsley, dried
- ➤ 1/2 tsp smoked paprika

Directions:

1. Toss the shrimp in a bowl with the oil, water, Tabasco sauce, pepper flakes, oregano, parsley, salt, pepper, and paprika.
2. Place the shrimp in an air fryer that has been prepared to 370 degrees F and cook for 10 minutes, shaking the fryer once.
3. Serve the shrimp on plates with a side salad. Enjoy!

Nutrition: 200 calories, 5 grams of fat, 6 grams of fiber, 13 grams of carbohydrates, and 8 grams of protein

Buttered Shrimp Skewers

Preparation time: 10 minutes **Cooking time:** 6 minutes
Servings: 2

Ingredients:

- ➤ 8 shrimps, peeled and deveined
- ➤ 4 garlic cloves, minced
- ➤ Salt and black pepper to the taste
- ➤ 8 green bell pepper slices
- ➤ 1 tbsp rosemary, chop
- ➤ 1 tbsp butter, melted

Directions:

1. Toss shrimp with garlic, butter, salt, pepper, rosemary, and bell pepper slices in a mixing basin to coat, then set aside for 10 minutes.
2. On a skewer, arrange 2 shrimp and 2 bell pepper slices, then repeat with the remaining shrimp and bell pepper slices.
3. Place them all in the basket of your air fryer and cook for 6 minutes at 360 degrees F.
4. Serve immediately after dividing among plates. Enjoy!

Nutrition: 140 calories, 1 gram of fat, 12 grams of fiber, 15 grams of carbohydrates, and 7 grams of protein

Asian Salmon

Preparation time: 1 hour **Cooking time:** 15 minutes
Servings: 2

Ingredients:

- ➤ 2 medium salmon fillets
- ➤ 6 tbsp light soy sauce
- ➤ 3 tsp mirin
- ➤ 1 tsp water
- ➤ 6 tbsp honey

Directions:

1. In a mixing dish, whisk together the soy sauce, honey, water, and mirin. Add the salmon, rub well, and chill for 1 hour.
2. Cook the salmon in your air fryer for 15 minutes at 360 degrees F, flipping after 7 minutes.
3. In the meantime, heat the soy marinade in a skillet over medium heat, stir thoroughly, and cook for 2 minutes before turning off the heat.
4. Serve the salmon on plates with the marinade drizzled all over it. Enjoy!

Nutrition: 300 calories, 12 grams of fat, 8 grams of fiber, 13 grams of carbohydrates, and 24 grams of protein

Cod Steaks with Plum Sauce

Preparation time: 10 minutes **Cooking time:** 20 minutes
Servings: 2

Ingredients:

- ➤ 2 big cod steaks
- ➤ Salt and black pepper to the taste

- ➢ 1/2 tsp garlic powder
- ➢ 1/2 tsp ginger powder
- ➢ 1/4 tsp turmeric powder
- ➢ 1 tbsp plum sauce
- ➢ Cooking spray

Directions:

1. Season the cod steaks with salt and pepper, then coat them in frying oil and massage with the garlic powder, ginger powder, and turmeric powder.
2. Cook the cod steaks in your air fryer for 15 minutes at 360 degrees F, flipping after 7 minutes.
3. Heat a pan over medium heat, then add the plum sauce and simmer for 2 minutes, stirring occasionally.
4. Serve fish steaks on plates with plum sauce drizzled over them. Enjoy

Nutrition: 250 calories, 7 grams of fat, 1 gram of fiber, 14 grams of carbohydrates, and 12 grams of protein

Flavored Air Fried Salmon

Preparation time: 1 hour **Cooking time:** 8 minutes
Servings: 2

Ingredients:

- ➢ 2 salmon fillets
- ➢ 2 tbsp lemon juice
- ➢ Salt and black pepper to the taste
- ➢ 1/2 tsp garlic powder
- ➢ 1/3 cup water

- ➤ 1/3 cup soy sauce
- ➤ 3 scallions, chop
- ➤ 1/3 cup brown sugar
- ➤ 2 tbsp olive oil

Directions:

1. In a mixing bowl, whisk together the sugar, water, soy sauce, garlic powder, salt, pepper, oil, and lemon juice. Add the salmon fillets, toss to coat, and chill for 1 hour.
2. Place the salmon fillets in the fryer basket and cook for 8 minutes at 360 degrees F, flipping halfway through.
3. Serve immediately by dividing the salmon between plates and sprinkling scallions on top. Enjoy!

Nutrition: 300 calories, 12 grams of fat, 10 grams of fiber, 23 grams of carbohydrates, and 20 grams of protein

Salmon with Capers and Mash

Preparation time: 10 minutes **Cooking time:** 20 minutes
Servings: 4

Ingredients:

- ➤ 4 salmon fillets, skinless and boneless
- ➤ 1 tbsp capers, drained
- ➤ Salt and black pepper to the taste
- ➤ Juice from 1 lemon
- ➤ 2 tsp olive oil

For the potato mash:

- ➤ 2 tbsp olive oil

- ➢ 1 tbsp dill, dried
- ➢ 1 pound potatoes, chop
- ➢ 1/2 cup milk

Directions:

1. Put potatoes in a pot, cover with water, season with salt, and bring to a boil over medium high heat for 15 minutes. Drain, transfer to a bowl, mash with a potato masher, add 2 tablespoons oil, dill, salt, pepper, and milk, mix well, and set aside.
2. Season salmon with salt and pepper, rub with 2 tablespoons oil, place to air fryer basket, top with capers, and cook for 8 minutes at 360 degrees F.
3. Serve salmon and capers on plates with mashed potatoes on the side and a drizzle of lemon juice. Enjoy!

Nutrition: 300 calories, 17 grams of fat, 8 grams of fiber, 12 grams of carbohydrates, and 18 grams of protein

Lemony Saba Fish

Preparation time: 10 minutes **Cooking time:** 8 minutes
Servings: 1

Ingredients:

- ➢ 4 Saba fish fillet, boneless
- ➢ Salt and black pepper to the taste
- ➢ 3 red chili pepper, chop
- ➢ 2 tbsp lemon juice
- ➢ 2 tbsp olive oil
- ➢ 2 tbsp garlic, minced

Directions:

1. Salt and pepper the fish fillets and place them in a basin.
2. Toss with the lemon juice, oil, chile, and garlic, then transfer the fish to your air fryer and cook for 8 minutes, flipping halfway through.
3. Serve with some fries and divide among plates. Enjoy!

Nutrition: 300 calories, 4 grams of fat, 8 grams of fiber, 15 grams of carbohydrates, 15 grams of protein

Asian Halibut

Preparation time: 30 minutes **Cooking time:** 10 minutes
Servings: 3

Ingredients:

- ➢ 1 pound halibut steaks
- ➢ 2/3 cup soy sauce
- ➢ 1/4 cup sugar
- ➢ 2 tbsp lime juice
- ➢ 1/2 cup mirin
- ➢ 1/4 tsp red pepper flakes, crushed
- ➢ 1/4 cup orange juice
- ➢ 1/4 tsp ginger, grated
- ➢ 1 garlic clove, minced

Directions:

1. Heat soy sauce in a pan over medium heat, then add mirin, sugar, lime and orange juice, pepper flakes, ginger,

and garlic, stirring constantly. Bring to a boil, then remove from heat.
2. Transfer half of the marinade to a mixing bowl, add the halibut, toss to coat, and chill for 30 minutes.
3. Cook the halibut in the air fryer for 10 minutes at 390 degrees F, flipping once.
4. Serve the halibut steaks hot, with the rest of the marinade drizzled over them. Enjoy!

Nutrition: 286 calories, 5 grams of fat, 12 grams of fiber, 14 grams of carbohydrates, and 23 grams of protein

Cod and Vinaigrette

Preparation time: 10 minutes **Cooking time:** 15 minutes **Servings:** 4

Ingredients:

- ➢ 4 cod fillets, skinless and boneless
- ➢ 12 cherry tomatoes, halved
- ➢ 8 black olives, pitted and roughly chop
- ➢ 2 tbsp lemon juice
- ➢ Salt and black pepper to the taste
- ➢ 2 tbsp olive oil
- ➢ Cooking spray
- ➢ 1 bunch basil, chop

Directions:

1. Season fish with salt and pepper to taste, then place in the basket of your air fryer and cook for 10 minutes at 360 degrees F, flipping after 5 minutes.

2. Meanwhile, heat the oil in a skillet over medium heat, then add the tomatoes, olives, and lemon juice, mix to combine, bring to a simmer, add the basil, salt, and pepper, and remove from heat.
3. Serve the fish on plates with a sprinkle of vinaigrette on top. Enjoy!

Nutrition: 300 calories, 5 grams of fat, 8 grams of fiber, 12 grams of carbohydrates, and 8 grams of protein

Shrimp and Crab Mix

Preparation time: 10 minutes **Cooking time:** 25 minutes
Servings: 4

Ingredients:

- 1/2 cup yellow onion, chop
- 1 cup green bell pepper, chop
- 1 cup celery, chop
- 1 pound shrimp, peeled and deveined
- 1 cup crabmeat, flaked
- 1 cup mayonnaise
- 1 tsp Worcestershire sauce
- Salt and black pepper to the taste
- 2 tbsp breadcrumbs
- 1 tbsp butter, melted
- 1 tsp sweet paprika

Directions:

1. Toss shrimp with crab meat, bell pepper, onion, mayo, celery, salt, pepper, and Worcestershire sauce in a bowl

until well combined, then move to an air fryer pan.
2. Place bread crumbs and paprika on top, add melted butter, and cook at 320 degrees F for 25 minutes, shaking halfway through.
3. Serve immediately after dividing among plates. Enjoy!

Nutrition: 200 calories, 13 grams of fat, 9 grams of fiber, 17 grams of carbohydrates, 19 grams of protein

Seafood Casserole

Preparation time: 10 minutes **Cooking time:** 40 minutes
Servings: 6

Ingredients:

- ➤ 6 tbsp butter
- ➤ 2 oz mushrooms, chop
- ➤ 1 small green bell pepper, chop
- ➤ 1 celery stalk, chop
- ➤ 2 garlic cloves, minced
- ➤ 1 small yellow onion, chop
- ➤ Salt and black pepper to the taste
- ➤ 4 tbsp flour
- ➤ 1/2 cup white wine
- ➤ 1 and 1/2 cups milk
- ➤ 1/2 cup heavy cream
- ➤ 4 sea scallops, sliced
- ➤ 4 oz haddock, skinless, boneless and cut into small pieces
- ➤ 4 oz lobster meat, already cooked and cut into small pieces
- ➤ 1/2 tsp mustard powder

- ➢ 1 tbsp lemon juice
- ➢ 1/3 cup bread crumbs
- ➢ Salt and black pepper to the taste
- ➢ 3 tbsp cheddar cheese, grated
- ➢ A handful parsley, chop
- ➢ 1 tsp sweet paprika

Directions:

1. Add bell pepper, mushrooms, celery, garlic, onion, and wine to a pan with 4 tbsp butter over medium high heat, stir, and simmer for 10 minutes.
2. Cook for 6 minutes after adding the flour, cream, and milk.
3. Stir in the lemon juice, salt, pepper, mustard powder, scallops, lobster meat, and haddock, then remove from the heat and transfer to an air fryer-safe pan.
4. Combine the remaining butter, bread crumbs, paprika, and cheese in a bowl and sprinkle over the seafood mixture.
5. Place pan in air fryer and cook for 16 minutes at 360 degrees F.
6. Serve with a sprinkling of parsley on top of each serving. Enjoy!

Nutrition: 270 calories, 32 grams of fat, 14 grams of fiber, 15 grams of carbohydrates, and 23 grams of protein

Creamy Coconut Chicken

Preparation time: 2 hours **Cooking time:** 25 minutes
Servings: 4

Ingredients:

- ➢ 4 big chicken legs
- ➢ 5 tsp turmeric powder
- ➢ 2 tbsp ginger, grated
- ➢ Salt and black pepper to the taste
- ➢ 4 tbsp coconut cream

Directions:

1. In a mixing dish, whisk together the cream, turmeric, ginger, salt, and pepper. Add the chicken pieces, toss well, and set aside for 2 hours.
2. Cook for 25 minutes at 370 degrees F in a preheated air fryer, then divide among plates and serve with a side salad. Enjoy!

Nutrition: 300 calories, 4 grams of fat, 12 grams of fiber, 22 grams of carbohydrates, and 20 grams of protein

Chinese Chicken Wings

Preparation time: 2 hours **Cooking time:** 15 minutes
Servings: 6

Ingredients:

- ➢ 16 chicken wings
- ➢ 2 tbsp honey
- ➢ 2 tbsp soy sauce
- ➢ Salt and black pepper to the taste
- ➢ 1/4 tsp white pepper
- ➢ 3 tbsp lime juice

Directions:

1. In a mixing bowl, whisk together honey, soy sauce, salt, black and white pepper, and lime juice. Add chicken pieces, stir to coat, and chill for 2 hours.
2. Transfer the chicken to your air fryer and cook for 6 minutes on each side at 370 degrees F, then increase the heat to 400 degrees F and cook for 3 minutes more.
3. Serve immediately. Enjoy!

Nutrition: calories 372, fat 9, fiber 10, carbs 37, protein 24

Herbed Chicken

Preparation time: 30 minutes **Cooking time:** 40 minutes
Servings: 4

Ingredients:

➢ 1 whole chicken
➢ Salt and black pepper to the taste
➢ 1 tsp garlic powder
➢ 1 tsp onion powder
➢ 1/2 tsp thyme, dried
➢ 1 tsp rosemary, dried
➢ 1 tbsp lemon juice
➢ 2 tbsp olive oil

Directions:

1. Season the chicken with salt and pepper, then rub it with thyme, rosemary, garlic powder, and onion powder before rubbing it with lemon juice and olive oil and setting it aside for 30 minutes.

2. Cook the chicken in your air fryer for 20 minutes on each side at 360 degrees F.
3. Allow the chicken to cool before carving and serving. Enjoy!

Nutrition: calories 390, fat 10, fiber 5, carbs 22, protein 20

Chicken Parmesan

Preparation time: 10 minutes **Cooking time:** 15 minutes
Servings: 4

Ingredients:

- ➤ 2 cups panko bread crumbs
- ➤ 1/4 cup parmesan, grated
- ➤ 1/2 tsp garlic powder
- ➤ 2 cups white flour
- ➤ 1 egg, whisked
- ➤ 1 and 1/2 pounds chicken cutlets, skinless and boneless
- ➤ Salt and black pepper to the taste
- ➤ 1 cup mozzarella, grated
- ➤ 2 cups tomato sauce
- ➤ 3 tbsp basil, chop

Directions:

1. Stir together panko, parmesan, and garlic powder in a mixing basin.
2. In a separate bowl, combine the flour and the egg.
3. Season the chicken with salt and pepper, then coat it in flour, egg mixture, and panko.

4. Cook the chicken pieces in your air fryer for 3 minutes on each side at 360 degrees F.
5. Transfer the chicken to a baking dish that fits in your air fryer, sprinkle with tomato sauce and mozzarella, and cook at 375 degrees F for 7 minutes.
6. Serve by dividing among dishes and sprinkling basil over top. Enjoy!

Nutrition: 304 calories, 12 grams of fat, 11 grams of fiber, 22 grams of carbohydrates, and 15 grams of protein

Mexican Chicken

Preparation time: 10 minutes **Cooking time:** 20 minutes
Servings: 4

Ingredients:

- ➤ 16 oz salsa verde
- ➤ 1 tbsp olive oil
- ➤ Salt and black pepper to the taste
- ➤ 1 pound chicken breast, boneless and skinless
- ➤ 1 and 1/2 cup Monterey Jack cheese, grated
- ➤ 1/4 cup cilantro, chop
- ➤ 1 tsp garlic powder

Directions:

1. Season the chicken with salt, pepper, and garlic powder, then spray it with olive oil and arrange it over the salsa verde in an air fryer-safe baking dish.
2. Place in your air fryer and cook for 20 minutes at 380 degrees F.

3. Cook for another 2 minutes after adding the cheese.
4. Serve immediately, divided among plates. Enjoy!

Nutrition: 340 calories, 18 grams of fat, 14 grams of fiber, 32 grams of carbohydrates, and 18 grams of protein

Creamy Chicken, Rice and Peas

Preparation time: 10 minutes **Cooking time:** 30 minutes
Servings: 4

Ingredients:

➤ 1 pound chicken breasts, skinless, boneless and cut into quarters
➤ 1 cup white rice, already cooked
➤ Salt and black pepper to the taste
➤ 1 tbsp olive oil
➤ 3 garlic cloves, minced
➤ 1 yellow onion, chop
➤ 1/2 cup white wine
➤ 1/4 cup heavy cream
➤ 1 cup chicken stock
➤ 1/4 cup parsley, chop
➤ 2 cups peas, frozen
➤ 1 and 1/2 cups parmesan, grated

Directions:

1. Season the chicken breasts with salt and pepper, then spray half of the oil over them, rub well, and place in the air fryer basket to cook for 6 minutes at 360 degrees F.

2. Heat the remaining oil in a skillet over medium high heat, then add the garlic, onion, wine, stock, salt, pepper, and heavy cream, stirring constantly. Bring to a simmer, then cook for 9 minutes.
3. Transfer chicken breasts to a heat-proof dish that will fit in your air fryer, stir with peas, rice, and cream mixture, sprinkle with parmesan and parsley, and cook at 420 degrees F for 10 minutes.
4. Serve immediately, divided among plates. Enjoy!

Nutrition: 313 calories, 12 grams of fat, 14 grams of fiber, 27 grams of carbohydrates, 44 grams of protein

Italian Chicken

Preparation time: 10 minutes **Cooking time:** 16 minutes
Servings: 4

Ingredients:

- ➢ 5 chicken thighs
- ➢ 1 tbsp olive oil
- ➢ 2 garlic cloves, minced
- ➢ 1 tbsp thyme, chop
- ➢ 1/2 cup heavy cream
- ➢ 3/4 cup chicken stock
- ➢ 1 tsp red pepper flakes, crushed
- ➢ 1/4 cup parmesan, grated
- ➢ 1/2 cup sun dried tomatoes
- ➢ 2 tbsp basil, chop
- ➢ Salt and black pepper to the taste

Directions:

1. Season the chicken with salt and pepper, massage with half of the oil, and cook for 4 minutes in a preheated air fryer at 350 degrees F.
2. Meanwhile, heat the remaining oil in a skillet over medium high heat, then add the thyme, garlic, pepper flakes, sun dried tomatoes, heavy cream, stock, parmesan, salt, and pepper, stirring constantly. Bring to a simmer, then remove from heat and transfer to an air fryer-safe dish.
3. Add the chicken thighs on top, place in the air fryer, and cook for 12 minutes at 320 degrees F.
4. Serve with basil sprinkled over top, divided among plates. Enjoy!

Nutrition: 272 calories, 9 grams of fat, 12 grams of fiber, 37 grams of carbohydrates, 23 grams of protein

Chinese Duck Legs

Preparation time: 10 minutes **Cooking time:** 36 minutes
Servings: 2

Ingredients:

➢ 2 duck legs
➢ 2 dried chilies, chop
➢ 1 tbsp olive oil
➢ 2 star anise
➢ 1 bunch spring onions, chop
➢ 4 ginger slices
➢ 1 tbsp oyster sauce
➢ 1 tbsp soy sauce
➢ 1 tsp sesame oil

➢ 14 oz water

➢ 1 tbsp rice wine

Directions:

1. Heat the oil in a skillet over medium high heat, then add the chili, star anise, sesame oil, rice wine, ginger, oyster sauce, soy sauce, and water, and cook for 6 minutes, stirring occasionally.
2. Toss in the spring onions and duck legs to coat, then move to a pan that fits your air fryer, place in the air fryer, and cook for 30 minutes at 370 degrees F.
3. Serve by dividing the mixture among plates. Enjoy!

Nutrition: 300 calories, 12 grams of fat, 12 grams of fiber, 26 grams of carbohydrates, and 18 grams of protein

Flavored Rib Eye Steak

Preparation time: 10 minutes **Cooking time:** 20 minutes
Servings: 4

Ingredients:

➢ 2 pounds rib eye steak

➢ Salt and black pepper to the taste

➢ 1 tbsp olive oil

For the rub:

➢ 3 tbsp sweet paprika

➢ 2 tbsp onion powder

➢ 2 tbsp garlic powder

- ➤ 1 tbsp brown sugar
- ➤ 2 tbsp oregano, dried
- ➤ 1 tbsp cumin, ground
- ➤ 1 tbsp rosemary, dried

Directions:

1. Combine paprika, onion and garlic powder, sugar, oregano, rosemary, salt, pepper, and cumin in a bowl, stir, and rub the mixture over the steak.
2. Season the steaks with salt and pepper, then massage them with the oil again before placing them in the air fryer and cooking for 20 minutes at 400 degrees F, flipping halfway through.
3. Transfer the steak to a cutting board, slice it thinly, and serve with a salad on the side. Enjoy!

Nutrition: 320 calories, 8 grams of fat, 7 grams of fiber, 22 grams of carbohydrates, and 21 grams of protein

Chinese Steak and Broccoli

Preparation time: 45 minutes **Cooking time:** 12 minutes
Servings: 4

Ingredients:

- ➤ 3/4 pound round steak, cut into strips
- ➤ 1 pound broccoli florets
- ➤ 1/3 cup oyster sauce
- ➤ 2 tsp sesame oil
- ➤ 1 tsp soy sauce
- ➤ 1 tsp sugar

- ➢ 1/3 cup sherry
- ➢ 1 tbsp olive oil
- ➢ 1 garlic clove, minced

Directions:

1. Combine sesame oil, oyster sauce, soy sauce, sherry, and sugar in a mixing bowl, stirring well. Add beef, toss, and set aside for 30 minutes.
2. Add the beef, broccoli, garlic, and oil to a pan that fits your air fryer, toss everything well, and cook at 380 degrees F for 12 minutes.
3. Serve by dividing the mixture among plates. Enjoy!

Nutrition: 330 calories, 12 grams of fat, 7 grams of fiber, 23 grams of carbohydrates, 23 grams of protein

Provencal Pork

Preparation time: 10 minutes **Cooking time:** 15 minutes
Servings: 2

Ingredients:

- ➢ 1 red onion, sliced
- ➢ 1 yellow bell pepper, cut into strips
- ➢ 1 green bell pepper, cut into strips
- ➢ Salt and black pepper to the taste
- ➢ 2 tsp Provencal herbs
- ➢ 1/2 tbsp mustard
- ➢ 1 tbsp olive oil
- ➢ 7 oz pork tenderloin

Directions:

1. Toss yellow bell pepper with green bell pepper, onion, salt, pepper, Provencal herbs, and half of the oil in a baking dish that fits your air fryer.
2. Season the pork with salt, pepper, mustard, and the remaining oil, mix well, and serve alongside the vegetables.
3. Put everything in the air fryer, cook for 15 minutes at 370 degrees F, then divide among plates and serve. Enjoy!

Nutrition: 300 calories, 8 grams of fat, 7 grams of fiber, 21 grams of carbohydrates, 23 grams of protein

Beef S trips with Snow Peas and Mushrooms

Preparation time: 10 minutes **Cooking time:** 22 minutes **Servings:** 2

Ingredients:

➢ 2 beef steaks, cut into strips
➢ Salt and black pepper to the taste
➢ 7 oz snow peas
➢ 8 oz white mushrooms, halved
➢ 1 yellow onion, cut into rings
➢ 2 tbsp soy sauce
➢ 1 tsp olive oil

Directions:

1. Whisk together the olive oil and soy sauce in a mixing dish, then throw in the beef strips.

2. Toss snow peas, onion, and mushrooms with salt, pepper, and oil in a separate dish, then transfer to a pan that fits your air fryer and cook for 16 minutes at 350 degrees F.
3. Add the beef strips to the pan as well, and cook for another 6 minutes at 400 degrees F.
4. Serve by dividing everything between plates. Enjoy!

Nutrition: 235 calories, 8 grams of fat, 2 grams of fiber, 22 grams of carbohydrates, 24 grams of protein

Garlic Lamb Chops

Preparation time: 10 minutes **Cooking time:** 10 minutes
Servings: 4

Ingredients:

- ➢ 3 tbsp olive oil
- ➢ 8 lamb chops
- ➢ Salt and black pepper to the taste
- ➢ 4 garlic cloves, minced
- ➢ 1 tbsp oregano, chop
- ➢ 1 tbsp coriander, chop

Directions:

1. Combine oregano, salt, pepper, oil, garlic, and lamb chops in a mixing dish and toss to coat.
2. Cook for 10 minutes at 400 degrees F in your air fryer with lamb chops.
3. Serve the lamb chops on plates with a side salad. Enjoy!

Nutrition: 231 calories, 7 grams of fat, 5 grams of fiber, 14 grams of carbohydrates, 23 grams of protein

Crispy Lamb

Preparation time: 10 minutes **Cooking time:** 30 minutes
Servings: 4

Ingredients:

- 1 tbsp bread crumbs
- 2 tbsp macadamia nuts, toasted and crushed
- 1 tbsp olive oil
- 1 garlic clove, minced
- 28 oz rack of lamb
- Salt and black pepper to the taste
- 1 egg,
- 1 tbsp rosemary, chop

Directions:

1. Combine the oil and garlic in a mixing dish and whisk thoroughly.
2. Salt and pepper the lamb and brush it with the oil.
3. In a separate bowl, combine the nuts, breadcrumbs, and rosemary.
4. In a separate bowl, whisk the egg thoroughly.
5. Cook at 360 degrees F for 25 minutes, then increase to 400 degrees F and cook for 5 minutes more. Dip lamb in egg, then in macadamia mix, then place in air fryer basket.
6. Serve immediately after dividing among plates. Enjoy!

Nutrition: 230 calories, 2 grams of fat, 2 grams of fiber, 10 grams of carbs, and 12 grams of protein

Indian Pork

Preparation time: 35 minutes **Cooking time:** 10 minutes
Servings: 4

Ingredients:

- ➢ 1 tsp ginger powder
- ➢ 2 tsp chili paste
- ➢ 2 garlic cloves, minced
- ➢ 14 oz pork chops, cubed
- ➢ 1 shallot, chop
- ➢ 1 tsp coriander, ground
- ➢ 7 oz coconut milk
- ➢ 2 tbsp olive oil
- ➢ 3 oz peanuts, ground
- ➢ 3 tbsp soy sauce
- ➢ Salt and black pepper to the taste

Directions:

1. Mix ginger with 1 teaspoon chili paste, half of the garlic, half of the soy sauce, and half of the oil in a mixing bowl, whisking constantly. Add the meat, combine, and set aside for 10 minutes.
2. Transfer the meat to the basket of your air fryer and cook for 12 minutes at 400 degrees F, flipping halfway through.
3. Meanwhile, heat the remaining oil in a skillet over medium high heat and add the shallot, remaining garlic, coriander, coconut milk, remaining peanuts, remaining chili paste, and remaining soy sauce, stirring constantly for 5 minutes.
4. Serve by dividing the pork between plates and sprinkling the coconut mixture on top. Enjoy!

Nutrition: 423 calories, 11 grams of fat, 4 grams of fiber, 42 grams of carbohydrates, and 18 grams of protein

Spinach Pie

Preparation time: 10 minutes **Cooking time:** 15 minutes **Servings:** 4

Ingredients:

- 7 oz flour
- 2 tbsp butter
- 7oz spinach
- 1 tbsp olive oil
- 2 eggs
- 2 tbsp milk
- 3 oz cottage cheese
- Salt and black pepper to the taste
- 1 yellow onion, chop

Directions:

1. Combine flour, butter, 1 egg, milk, salt, and pepper in a food processor and process until smooth. Transfer to a bowl, knead, cover, and set aside for 10 minutes.
2. Over medium high heat, heat the oil in a pan, then add the onion and spinach, stir, and cook for 2 minutes.
3. Season with salt and pepper, then whisk in the remaining egg and cottage cheese before turning off the heat.
4. Divide dough into four parts, roll each piece, place on the bottom of a ramekin, top with spinach filling, place

ramekins in air fryer basket, and cook for 15 minutes at 360 degrees F.
5. Enjoy while it's hot!

Nutrition: 250 calories, 12 grams of fat, 2 grams of fiber, 23 grams of carbohydrates, and 12 grams of protein

Balsamic Artichokes

Preparation time: 10 minutes **Cooking time:** 7 minutes
Servings: 4

Ingredients:

- 4 big artichokes, trimmed
- Salt and black pepper to the taste
- 2 tbsp lemon juice
- 1/4 cup extra virgin olive oil
- 2 tsp balsamic vinegar
- 1 tsp oregano, dried
- 2 garlic cloves, minced

Directions:

1. Season artichokes with salt and pepper, then rub half of the oil and half of the lemon juice on them before placing them in your air fryer and cooking for 7 minutes at 360 degrees F.
2. Meanwhile, whisk together the remaining lemon juice, vinegar, remaining oil, salt, pepper, garlic, and oregano in a mixing bowl.
3. Arrange the artichokes on a dish and serve with the balsamic vinaigrette. Enjoy!

Nutrition: 200 calories, 3 grams of fat, 6 grams of fiber, 12 grams of carbohydrates, and 4 grams of protein

Cheesy Artichokes

Preparation time: 10 minutes **Cooking time:** 6 minutes
Servings: 6

Ingredients:

- 14 oz canned artichoke hearts
- 8 oz cream cheese
- 16 oz parmesan cheese, grated
- 10 oz spinach
- 1/2 cup chicken stock
- 8 oz mozzarella, shredded
- 1/2 cup sour cream
- 3 garlic cloves, minced
- 1/2 cup mayonnaise
- 1 tsp onion powder

Directions:

1. Toss artichokes with stock, garlic, spinach, cream cheese, sour cream, onion powder, and mayo in a pan that fits your air fryer, toss, and cook at 350 degrees F for 6 minutes.
2. Serve with mozzarella and parmesan cheeses. Enjoy!

Nutrition: 261 calories, 12 grams of fat, 2 grams of fiber, 12 grams of carbohydrates, and 15 grams of protein

Artichokes and Special Sauce

Preparation time: 10 minutes **Cooking time:** 6 minutes
Servings: 2

Ingredients:

- ➤ 2 artichokes, trimmed
- ➤ A drizzle of olive oil
- ➤ 2 garlic cloves, minced
- ➤ 1 tbsp lemon juice

For the sauce:

- ➤ 1/4 cup coconut oil
- ➤ 1/4 cup extra virgin olive oil
- ➤ 3 anchovy fillets
- ➤ 3 garlic cloves

Directions:

1. Toss artichokes with oil, 2 garlic cloves, and lemon juice in a bowl until well combined, then place to your air fryer and cook for 6 minutes at 350 degrees F. Divide among plates.
2. Blend coconut oil, anchovies, 3 garlic cloves, and olive oil in a food processor until smooth. Drizzle over artichokes and serve. Enjoy!

Nutrition: 261 calories, 4 grams of fat, 7 grams of fiber, 20 grams of carbohydrates, and 12 grams of protein

Beet Salad and Parsley Dressing

Preparation time: 10 minutes **Cooking time:** 14 minutes
Servings: 4

Ingredients:

- ➢ 4 beets
- ➢ 2 tbsp balsamic vinegar
- ➢ A bunch of parsley, chop
- ➢ Salt and black pepper to the taste
- ➢ 1 tbsp extra virgin olive oil
- ➢ 1 garlic clove, chop
- ➢ 2 tbsp capers

Directions:

1. Cook the beets in your air fryer for 14 minutes at 360 degrees F.
2. Meanwhile, combine parsley, garlic, salt, pepper, olive oil, and capers in a mixing dish and whisk well.
3. Transfer the beets to a chopping board, set aside to cool, then peel, slice, and serve in a salad dish.
4. Serve with vinegar and a parsley dressing drizzled over the top. Enjoy!

Nutrition: 70 calories, 2 grams of fat, 1 gram of fiber, 6 grams of carbohydrates, and 4 grams of protein

Beets and Blue Cheese Salad

Preparation time: 10 minutes **Cooking time:** 14 minutes
Servings: 6

Ingredients:

- ➢ 6 beets, peeled and quartered
- ➢ Salt and black pepper to the taste
- ➢ 1/4 cup blue cheese, crumbled
- ➢ 1 tbsp olive oil

Directions:

1. Cook the beets in your air fryer for 14 minutes at 350 degrees F before transferring them to a bowl.
2. Toss in the blue cheese, salt, pepper, and oil before serving. Enjoy!

Nutrition: 100 calories, 4 grams of fat, 4 grams of fiber, 10 grams of carbohydrates, 5 grams of protein

Beet s and Arugula Salad

Preparation time: 10 minutes **Cooking time:** 10 minutes **Servings:** 4

Ingredients:

- ➢ 1 and 1/2 pounds beets, peeled and quartered
- ➢ A drizzle of olive oil
- ➢ 2 tsp orange zest, grated
- ➢ 2 tbsp cider vinegar
- ➢ 1/2 cup orange juice
- ➢ 2 tbsp brown sugar
- ➢ 2 scallions, chop
- ➢ 2 tsp mustard
- ➢ 2 cups arugula

Directions:

1. Rub the beets with the oil and orange juice, then place them in the air fryer and cook for 10 minutes at 350 degrees F.
2. Toss beet quarters with onions, arugula, and orange zest in a bowl.
3. In a small dish, whisk together the sugar, mustard, and vinegar. Add to the salad, stir, and serve. Enjoy!

Nutrition: 121 calories, 2 grams of fat, 3 grams of fiber, 11 grams of carbohydrates, 4 grams of protein

Beet , Tomato and Goat Cheese Mix

Preparation time: 30 minutes **Cooking time:** 14 minutes **Servings:** 8

Ingredients:

➢ 8 small beets, trimmed, peeled and halved
➢ 1 red onion, sliced
➢ 4 oz goat cheese, crumbled
➢ 1 tbsp balsamic vinegar
➢ Salt and black pepper to the taste
➢ 2 tbsp sugar
➢ 1 pint mixed cherry tomatoes, halved
➢ 2 oz pecans
➢ 2 tbsp olive oil

Directions:

1. Place the beets in the air fryer, season with salt and pepper, and cook for 14 minutes at 350 degrees F before transferring to a salad dish.

2. Toss in the onion, cherry tomatoes, and pecans.
3. In a separate dish, whisk together the vinegar, sugar, and oil until the sugar dissolves, then add to the salad.
4. Toss in the goat cheese and serve. Enjoy!

Nutrition: 124 calories, 7 grams of fat, 5 grams of fiber, 12 grams of carbohydrates, and 6 grams of protein

Tasty Banana Cake

Preparation time: 10 minutes **Cooking time:** 30 minutes
Servings: 4

Ingredients:

- ➢ 1 tbsp butter, soft
- ➢ 1 egg
- ➢ 1/3 cup brown sugar
- ➢ 2 tbsp honey
- ➢ 1 banana, peeled and mashed
- ➢ 1 cup white flour
- ➢ 1 tsp baking powder
- ➢ 1/2 tsp cinnamon powder
- ➢ Cooking spray

Directions:

1. Set aside a cake pan that has been sprayed with cooking spray.
2. Whisk together butter, sugar, banana, honey, egg, cinnamon, baking powder, and flour in a mixing dish.
3. Pour the mixture into a greased cake pan, place it in your air fryer, and cook for 30 minutes at 350 degrees F.

4. Allow the cake to cool before slicing and serving. Enjoy!

Nutrition: 232 calories, 4 grams of fat, 1 gram of fiber, 34 grams of carbohydrates, and 4 grams of protein

Simple Cheesecake

Preparation time: 10 minutes **Cooking time:** 15 minutes
Servings: 15

Ingredients:

- ➢ 1 pound cream cheese
- ➢ 1/2 tsp vanilla extract
- ➢ 2 eggs
- ➢ 4 tbsp sugar
- ➢ 1 cup graham crackers, crumbled
- ➢ 2 tbsp butter

Directions:

1. Combine crackers and butter in a mixing basin.
2. Place the crackers mix in the bottom of a lined cake pan, place in the air fryer, and cook for 4 minutes at 350 degrees F.
3. Meanwhile, whisk together the sugar, cream cheese, eggs, and vanilla in a mixing dish.
4. Spread the filling over the cracker crust and bake for 15 minutes at 310 degrees F in your air fryer.
5. Refrigerate the cake for 3 hours before slicing and serving. Enjoy!

Nutrition: 245 calories, 12 grams of fat, 1 gram of fiber, 20 grams of carbohydrates, 3 grams of protein

Bread Pudding

Preparation time: 10 minutes **Cooking time:** 1 hour
Servings: 4

Ingredients:

- ➤ 6 glazed doughnuts, crumbled
- ➤ 1 cup cherries
- ➤ 4 egg yolks
- ➤ 1 and 1/2 cups whipping cream
- ➤ 1/2 cup raisins
- ➤ 1/4 cup sugar
- ➤ 1/2 cup chocolate chips.

Directions:

1. Combine cherries, egg yolks, and whipping cream in a mixing basin and stir thoroughly.
2. In a separate bowl, combine together the raisins, sugar, chocolate chips, and doughnuts.
3. Combine the two mixtures, transfer to a greased pan that fits your air fryer, and bake for 1 hour at 310 degrees F.
4. Before cutting and serving the pudding, chill it. Enjoy!

Nutrition: 302 calories, 8 grams of fat, 2 grams of fiber, 23 grams of carbohydrates, 10 grams of protein

Bread Dough and Amaretto Dessert

Preparation time: 10 minutes **Cooking time:** 12 minutes
Servings: 12

Ingredients:

- ➢ 1 pound bread dough
- ➢ 1 cup sugar
- ➢ 1/2 cup butter, melted
- ➢ 1 cup heavy cream
- ➢ 12 oz chocolate chips
- ➢ 2 tbsp amaretto liqueur

Directions:

1. Roll out the dough and cut it into 20 pieces, then half each slice.
2. Brush dough pieces with butter, sprinkle with sugar, and set them in your air fryer's basket after brushing it with butter. Cook for 5 minutes at 350 degrees F, turn, and cook for another 3 minutes before transferring to a platter.
3. Heat the heavy cream in a skillet over medium heat, then add the chocolate chips and stir until they melt.
4. Stir in the liquor, then transfer to a bowl and serve with bread dippers. Enjoy!

Nutrition: 200 calories, 1 gram fat, 0 gram fiber, 6 gram carbohydrates, 6 gram protein

Cinnamon Rolls and Cream Cheese Dip

Preparation time: 2 hours **Cooking time:** 15 minutes
Servings: 8

Ingredients:

- ➢ 1 pound bread dough

- ➤ 3/4 cup brown sugar
- ➤ 1 and 1/2 tbsp cinnamon, ground
- ➤ 1/4 cup butter, melted

For the cream cheese dip:

- ➤ 2 tbsp butter
- ➤ 4 oz cream cheese
- ➤ 1 and 1/4 cups sugar
- ➤ 1/2 tsp vanilla

Directions:

1. On a floured work surface, roll out the dough into a rectangle and brush with 1/4 cup butter.
2. Combine cinnamon and sugar in a bowl, stir to combine, and sprinkle over dough. Roll dough into a log, seal well, and cut into 8 pieces.
3. Allow rolls to rise for 2 hours before placing them in the air fryer basket and cooking for 5 minutes at 350 degrees F, flipping them and cooking for another 4 minutes before transferring to a platter.
4. Combine cream cheese, butter, sugar, and vanilla in a mixing dish and whisk thoroughly.
5. Serve this cream cheese dip with your cinnamon buns. Enjoy!

Nutrition: 200 calories, 1 gram fat, 0 gram fiber, 5 gram carbohydrates, 6 gram protein

Pumpkin Pie

Preparation time: 10 minutes **Cooking time:** 15 minutes
Servings: 9

Ingredients:

- ➢ 1 tbsp sugar
- ➢ 2 tbsp flour
- ➢ 1 tbsp butter
- ➢ 2 tbsp water

For the pumpkin pie filling:

- ➢ 3.5 oz pumpkin flesh, chop
- ➢ 1 tsp mixed spice
- ➢ 1 tsp nutmeg
- ➢ 3 oz water
- ➢ 1 egg, whisked
- ➢ 1 tbsp sugar

Directions:

1. 3 oz water in a pot over medium high heat, bring to a boil, add pumpkin, egg, 1 tbsp sugar, spice, and nutmeg, stir, cook for 20 minutes, remove from heat, and puree with an immersion blender.
2. Combine flour, butter, 1 tablespoon sugar, and 2 tablespoons water in a mixing basin and knead your dough thoroughly.
3. Butter a pie pan that will fit in your air fryer, push dough into the pan, fill with pumpkin pie filling, set in the air fryer's basket, and cook for 15 minutes at 360 degrees F.
4. Slice and serve while still warm. Enjoy!

Nutrition: 200 calories, 5 grams of fat, 2 grams of fiber, 5 grams of carbohydrates, 6 grams of protein

Wrapped Pears

Preparation time: 10 minutes **Cooking time:** 15 minutes
Servings: 4

Ingredients:

- ➢ 4 puff pastry sheets
- ➢ 14 oz vanilla custard
- ➢ 2 pears, halved
- ➢ 1 egg, whisked
- ➢ 1/2 tsp cinnamon powder
- ➢ 2 tbsp sugar

Directions:

1. Place puff pastry pieces on a work surface, top with spoonfuls of vanilla custard, pear halves, and wrap.
2. Brush pears with egg, sugar, and cinnamon, then set them in the basket of your air fryer and cook for 15 minutes at 320 degrees F.
3. Serve by dividing the parcels among plates. Enjoy!

Nutrition: 200 calories, 2 grams of fat, 1 gram of fiber, 14 grams of carbohydrates, 3 grams of protein

Strawberry Donuts

Preparation time: 10 minutes **Cooking time:** 15 minutes
Servings: 4

Ingredients:

- ➢ 8 oz flour
- ➢ 1 tbsp brown sugar
- ➢ 1 tbsp white sugar

- ➤ 1 egg
- ➤ 2 and 1/2 tbsp butter
- ➤ 4 oz whole milk
- ➤ 1 tsp baking powder

For the strawberry icing:

- ➤ 2 tbsp butter
- ➤ 3.5 oz icing sugar
- ➤ 1/2 tsp pink coloring
- ➤ 1/4 cup strawberries, chop
- ➤ 1 tbsp whipped cream

Directions:

1. Stir butter, 1 tablespoon brown sugar, 1 tablespoon white sugar, and flour together in a mixing basin.
2. In a separate bowl, whisk together the egg, 1 1/2 tablespoons butter, and milk.
3. Combine the two mixtures, stir, and form donuts out of the mixture in your air fryer basket. Cook for 15 minutes at 360 degrees F.
4. Whisk together 1 tablespoon of butter, icing sugar, food coloring, whipped cream, and strawberry puree.
5. Serve doughnuts with strawberry icing on top on a tray. Enjoy!

Nutrition: 250 calories, 12 grams of fat, 1 gram of fiber, 32 grams of carbohydrates, and 4 grams of protein

Air Fried Bananas

Preparation time: 10 minutes **Cooking time:** 15 minutes
Servings: 4

Ingredients:

- ➢ 3 tbsp butter
- ➢ 2 eggs
- ➢ 8 bananas, peeled and halved
- ➢ 1/2 cup corn flour
- ➢ 3 tbsp cinnamon sugar
- ➢ 1 cup panko

Directions:

1. Heat the butter in a pan over medium high heat, then add the panko, mix, and cook for 4 minutes before transferring to a bowl.
2. Roll each in the flour, egg, and panko mixture, place in the air fryer basket, dust with cinnamon sugar, and cook for 10 minutes at 280 degrees F.
3. Serve immediately. Enjoy!

Nutrition: 164 calories, 1 gram of fat, 4 grams of fiber, 32 grams of carbohydrates, and 4 grams of protein

Cocoa Cake

Preparation time: 10 minutes **Cooking time:** 17 minutes
Servings: 6

Ingredients:

- ➢ 3.5 oz butter, melted
- ➢ 3 eggs

- ➤ 3 oz sugar
- ➤ 1 tsp cocoa powder
- ➤ 3 oz flour
- ➤ 1/2 tsp lemon juice

Directions:

1. 1 tbsp butter + 1 tbsp cocoa powder + 1 tbsp flour + 1 tbsp flour + 1 tbsp flour + 1 tbs
2. In a separate bowl, whisk together the remaining butter, sugar, eggs, flour, and lemon juice. Pour half of the batter into an air fryer-safe cake pan.
3. Spread half of the cocoa mix on top, then apply the remaining butter layer and the remaining cocoa.
4. Cook at 360°F for 17 minutes in an air fryer.
5. Before slicing and serving, let the cake to cool down. Enjoy!

Nutrition: 340 calories, 11 grams of fat, 3 grams of fiber, 25 grams of carbohydrates, and 5 grams of protein

Chocolate Cake

Preparation time: 10 minutes **Cooking time:** 30 minutes
Servings: 12

Ingredients:

- ➤ 3/4 cup white flour
- ➤ 3/4 cup whole wheat flour
- ➤ 1 tsp baking soda
- ➤ 3/4 tsp pumpkin pie spice
- ➤ 3/4 cup sugar

- ➤ 1 banana, mashed
- ➤ 1/2 tsp baking powder
- ➤ 2 tbsp canola oil
- ➤ 1/2 cup Greek yogurt
- ➤ 8 oz canned pumpkin puree
- ➤ Cooking spray
- ➤ 1 egg
- ➤ 1/2 tsp vanilla extract
- ➤ 2/3 cup chocolate chips

Directions:

1. Combine white flour, whole wheat flour, salt, baking soda and powder, and pumpkin spice in a mixing bowl and stir to combine.
2. Mix sugar, oil, banana, yogurt, pumpkin puree, vanilla, and egg in a separate bowl with a mixer.
3. Combine the two batters, toss in the chocolate chips, and pour into a prepared Bundt pan that will fit in your air fryer.
4. Cook for 30 minutes at 330 degrees Fahrenheit in your air fryer.
5. Allow the cake to cool completely before slicing and serving. Enjoy!

Nutrition: 232 calories, 7 grams of fat, 7 grams of fiber, 29 grams of carbohydrates, and 4 grams of protein

Apple Bread

Preparation time: 10 minutes **Cooking time:** 40 minutes
Servings: 6

Ingredients:

- ➢ 3 cups apples, cored and cubed
- ➢ 1 cup sugar
- ➢ 1 tbsp vanilla
- ➢ 2 eggs
- ➢ 1 tbsp apple pie spice
- ➢ 2 cups white flour
- ➢ 1 tbsp baking powder
- ➢ 1 stick butter
- ➢ 1 cup water

Directions:

1. In a mixing bowl, whisk together the egg, 1 butter stick, apple pie spice, and sugar using an electric mixer.
2. Stir in the apples thoroughly.
3. In a separate dish, whisk together the baking powder and flour.
4. Mix the two mixes together, then pour into a spring form pan.
5. Cook for 40 minutes at 320 degrees F in an air fryer with a spring form pan.
6. Cut into slices and serve. Enjoy!

Nutrition: 192 calories, 6 grams of fat, 7 grams of fiber, 14 grams of carbohydrates, and 7 grams of protein

Banana Bread

Preparation time: 10 minutes **Cooking time:** 40 minutes
Servings: 6

Ingredients:

- 3/4 cup sugar
- 1/3 cup butter
- 1 tsp vanilla extract
- 1 egg
- 2 bananas, mashed
- 1 tsp baking powder
- 1 and 1/2 cups flour
- 1/2 tsp baking soda
- 1/3 cup milk
- 1 and 1/2 tsp cream of tartar
- Cooking spray

Directions:

1. Stir together milk, cream of tartar, sugar, butter, egg, vanilla, and bananas in a mixing dish.
2. Combine flour, baking powder, and baking soda in a separate bowl.
3. Combine the two mixtures, whisk well, pour into a cake pan sprayed with cooking spray, place in the air fryer, and cook for 40 minutes at 320 degrees F.
4. Remove the bread from the oven, set it aside to cool, then slice and serve. Enjoy!

Nutrition: 292 calories, 7 grams of fat, 8 grams of fiber, 28 grams of carbohydrates, and 4 grams of protein

Printed in Great Britain
by Amazon